森林海中的紅樓
Red Chamber in the Concrete Forest

編劇 **王昊然**
Playwright **Wang Haoran**

英文翻譯 **張菁**
English Translation **Gigi Chang**

香港藝術節委約及製作
Commissioned & produced by the Hong Kong Arts Festival

前言

第 42 屆香港藝術節匯聚了各式各樣的英雄：愛國的綠林與打虎英雄、力抗社會規範的戀人、穿着閃亮盔甲的神秘武士，以及玩命的魔術師。舞蹈與音樂方面亦有勇於突破的英雄。眾多的英雄還包括香港兩位年輕編劇，您不但能在舞台上看到他們的作品，亦可在本書細細欣賞。

自藝術節開始製作及出版本地劇場作品以來，一直主要以中文及粵語為媒介。今年，我們委約了首個英文劇本，探討在這雙語城市中向來遭受忽略的一群。我希望今後會有更多這類作品。

我謹向兩位編劇王昊然及楊靜安致意，還有眾多為第 42 屆香港藝術節獻藝的藝術工作者。感謝我們的觀眾、合作夥伴及支持者，您們的支持對藝術節不可或缺。最後，還要感謝藝術節的同事，你們的幹勁與熱誠令我明白到何謂平凡的英雄，與你們共事乃我的光榮。

何嘉坤
香港藝術節行政總監

Foreword

The 42nd HKAF is filled with heroes: patriotic outlaws and a tiger-quelling young warrior, lovers fighting societal norms, a mysterious knight in shining armour, and a doubtful death-defying magician. There are also heroes of dance and heroic journeys in music. In this company of heroes, we must count two young playwrights whose work you can enjoy both on stage and in the pages that follow.

Since embarking on production and publication of local theatre, we have worked exclusively in Chinese thus far. This year, we mark another milestone in doing the first English language production, addressing a sector that is somewhat underserved in a bilingual city. I hope that other works will follow in the years to come.

I salute both playwrights: Wang Haoran and Young Jingan, and the many artists whose talent and artistry lend lustre to the 42nd HKAF. I also salute our audiences and the many partners and supporters whose contributions make the Festival possible. Above all, I salute my HKAF colleagues. Their energy and dedication inform my understanding of what it means to be a hero on a daily basis, and it is a privilege to be in their company.

Tisa Ho

Executive Director, Hong Kong Arts Festival

編劇的話

來到香港的第一年，我租下了灣仔區一間十平方米不到的套房，七樓，沒電梯，3400 人民幣一個月。為了省下網費，我敲了鄰居的門，是一位胖胖的菲律賓姐姐，她只穿着睡衣和內褲。她對我笑，我問她願意一起分攤網費嗎？於是她留下了電話，她叫 Amy。後來，常碰見她房間出入不同的白人和聽見晚上傳來的聲音，我才知道她是一名性工作者，香港人稱之鳳姐。

一個深夜，我出去跑步，因為這時間沒車沒人。回來時發現沒帶鑰匙，我冷得要死，而該死的房東不肯幫忙，他只會用我聽不懂的潮州話罵我。我撥通 Amy 的號碼，不一會兒，穿着睡衣和內褲的 Amy 噔噔噔跑下來開門了，咯咯地笑我。終於明白了什麼叫遠親不如近鄰，Amy 是我在香港的第一個朋友。

兩年後我搬到了旺角，全球人口最密集的區域。在我的樓下，住了十幾個鳳姐，賓客往來，絡繹不絕，她們幾乎都是內地來的移民，香港的小夥子和大叔們十分喜愛光顧，甚至某些房間門口有客人排隊等候。我所見的是，上來的每個香港同胞都帶着一臉惆悵或是焦慮，出來時，腳下都帶着一股清風，飄然而去。不一會，出現一兩名鳳姐，嗒嗒的高跟鞋經過走廊，帶着一種幹練和自信消失在另一個房間。香港的朋友總愛提中港矛盾，而每當此時，我實在不曉得這矛盾究竟在何處。

有感於城市森林裏這一點如燈塔般溫暖的紅光，我寫下了《森林海中的紅樓》。

王昊然

2014 年 1 月 28 日

王昊然
Wang Haoran

香港演藝學院戲劇藝術碩士(優異),深圳大學英文文學學士(輔修日語)。
編劇作品有《桎梏》、《叉燒》(新域劇團劇場裏的臥虎與藏龍)、
《爆‧蛹》(第41屆香港藝術節)等,另著多部短劇,其中憑《我不是
Woyzeck》獲2013年由美國愛荷華大學和上海話劇藝術中心聯合舉辦
的「劇翼」國際寫作計劃一等獎。

導演作品有《螳螂捕蟬》、《菲德拉的愛》和《作家之死》等。主演劇目
包括《威尼斯商人》、《沃依采克》、《金尾小恐龍》等。普通話翻譯作
品有《示範單位》(潘惠森著)、《香港式離婚》(黃詠詩著)、中文翻譯
作品有《茱莉小姐》(艾瑤‧花柏改編)、《末族》(楊靜安著)等。

Wang graduated from the Hong Kong Academy for Performing
Arts (HKAPA) with a Master of Fine Arts in Drama (Distinction).
He also holds a bachelor's degree from Shenzhen University, where
he majored in English literature and minored in Japanese. His plays
include *Shackle*, *The Barbecued Pork* (Prospect Theatre), *Blast* (The 41th
Hong Kong Arts Festival), and others. He has authored a number of
short plays including *I'm Not Woyzeck*, first-prize winner in The Book
Wing 2013 (Drama) co-presented by the Iowa University and Shanghai
Dramatic Arts Centre. Wang has directed various productions, such
as *To Kill or to be Killed*, *Phaedra's Love*, *Death of a Writer* and others. He
has played the lead roles in *The Merchant of Venice*, *Woyzeck*, *The Little
Dinosaur with a Golden Tail*, and other productions. He has translated
the following scripts into Chinese versions, including *Show Flat* (Poon
Wai-sum), *The Truth About Lying* (Wong Wing-sze), *Mies Julie* (adapted
by Yaël Farber), *FILTH* (Jingan Macpherson Young).

《森林海中的紅樓》首演於第 42 屆香港藝術節，
2014 年 2 月 28 日，香港文化中心劇場

Red Chamber in the Concrete Forest premiered at the Studio
Theatre, Hong Kong Cultural Centre, 28 February, 2014,
42nd Hong Kong Arts Festival

編劇 Playwright
王臭然 Wang Haoran

導演 Director
陳曙曦 Chan Chu Hei

佈景及服裝設計 Set and Costume Designer
葉卓棠 Moon Yip Cheuk Tong

燈光設計 Lighting Designer
黃宇恒 Bert Wong

音樂及音響設計 Music and Sound Designer
梁寶榮 Leung Po Wing

製作經理 Production Manager
陳淡疇 Amum Chan

監製 Producer
香港藝術節 Hong Kong Arts Festival

角色及首演演出 Characters and Premiere Cast

男子 鄧世昌
Man Tang Sai Cheong

少女 張君泇
Girl Sheena Cheung

李可 許晉邦
Li Ke Hui Chun Pong

秦蕓 趙伊禕
Qin Yun Zhao Yiyi

少年 陳瑋聰
Boy Anson Chan Wai Chung

汪靜 勞燕
Wang Jing Sarah Lao

三段對風塵女子的憐惜，一名少年的逐步蛻變。

男子 — 等待綜援的失業者，三十來歲。
少女 — 男子的網友。
李可 — 保險銷售兼補習社老師，二十來歲。
秦薔 — 在港漂泊的福建籍女子，二十來歲。
少年 — 中學畢業生。
汪靜 — 在港漂泊的湖南籍女子，三十來歲。

註： 秦薔說略帶口音的廣東話，但並不嚴重，說普通話時以
　　（國）註明；
　　汪靜說普通話，說廣東話時以（粵）註明；
　　其餘角色語言皆為廣東話。

「／」 代表本句對白進行時下一句對白的起始位置。
「—」 代表本句對白被下一句對白打斷的位置。
「…」 代表人物暗示、猶豫或思考時台詞的漸弱。

第一場　私會

第一場　私會

時間：春天的某個深夜。
地點：男子的居所。
人物：男子、少女。

【一間普通的套房】
【一名男子，在佈置些什麼】
【他站在凳子上，打開壁櫥，手中拿著一支紅酒和一瓶Vodka，在考慮著什麼】
【他將紅酒收進壁櫥，將 Vodka 放進冰箱，同時看了看錶】
【他拿出一支香水往身上噴了噴】
【他坐進沙發，放起了音樂】
【他將兩個喇叭抱在耳邊陶醉】
【隱約傳來敲門聲，他沒有發覺】
【忽地，他不再陶醉，起身開門】
【門口出現一名學生模樣的文靜少女】
女：Hi.
【停頓】
男：Hi...
【停頓】
【忽地，男子意識到該讓少女進門，他退到一旁】
【少女入，準備脫鞋】
男：唔使㗎嘞。
【男子關上門】

女：唔，你特登噴香水添呀？—

【少女湊近聞】

女：Boss？

男：……

女：Dunhill？

男：……

女：Dior？Davidoff？Versace？—

男：我……是但噴㗎咋。

女：……

男：坐，飲啲咩？

【少女準備坐沙發，看到窗上的壁虎】

女：哇！咩嚟㗎？！

男：噢，冇事㗎……

女：好肥嘅蜥蜴呀！

男：係檐蛇。

女：咩話？

男：檐蛇，壁虎呀。

女：可以整走佢嗎？

男：死咗唔識郁㗎喇。

【男子翻動冰箱】

男：飲啲咩？

【少女坐在沙發對面的圓凳上】

男：檸檬茶？梳打水？

女：……

男：咖啡？奶茶？檸樂？檸水？

女：是但啦。

男：我度仲有啲餅你要唔要？

女：你……覺得我點呀？

男：吓？

女：靚唔靚？

【停頓】

男：呵，咁直接嘅你 ─

女：你唔係第一日識我喇嘛。

男：都算㗎，第一次見吖嘛。

【少女看了看手錶】

【男人從冰箱拿出月餅和酒，擺在茶几上】

女：點解隻檐蛇死係嗰度？

男：呵，曬死。

女：曬死？

男：佢唔覺意黐實咗喺個窗度 ─

女：咦……

男：你睇真啲，佢條尾仲斷開咗添 ─

女：可以整走佢嗎？

【停頓】

女：唔該。

【男子拉上窗簾】

男：咁咪 OK 囉。

女：你放啲咩音樂？

男：Coldplay ─

女：唱嚟唱去都差唔多咁嘅 ─

男：我至鍾意loop呢隻曲 —

女：可以校細聲啲嗎？

男：Sorry.

【男子調至靜音】

女：Thank you. 咩黎㗎？

男：……餅。

女：……月餅？

男：……都係餅啫。

女：宜家三月頭咋喎……

男：Sorry 屋企得呢樣，食得㗎……仲 —

【停頓】

【少女從手袋內拿出手機，隨手看了看錶】

【男子望了望少女】

男：啊，你睇上去唔多似。

女：（笑）吓？

男：你微信俾我啲相張張都……影到成個 Angelababy 咁……

女：宜家呢？

男：你……似啲中學生……

【沉默】

女：企起身。

【停頓】

女：企啦。

【男子起，少女擁抱男子】

【一陣，鬆開】

女：（溫柔地）放鬆啲，唔好咁緊張。

13

【少女坐下】

女：仲企響度做咩？坐啦。

【男子坐下】

女：好啲未？

男：吓？

女：睇你個樣唔係空虛就係失戀。

男：你幾歲呀？

女：你估？

男：呵。

女：哈，好特別呀。

男：我呀？

女：攞月餅同 Vodka 嚟招呼我。

男：啊，sorry，杯都未攞出嚟添。

【男子找出一隻大碗，推到少女面前】

男：唔好意思搵唔到杯。

女：俾杯水我吖，唔該。

【男子倒了一碗水給少女】

女：乜我個樣好細咩？

男：似啫，就算你有 BB 都唔出奇。

女：你點知嘅？

男：……吓？

女：我仲講咗啲咩吖？

【停頓】

男：你仲話——

女：BB 真係好麻煩㗎——

男：……

女：你要睇住佢食，睇住佢屙一

男：我明。

女：重要睇住佢唔好咬親人 一

男：明……吓？

【停頓】

女：BB 係我隻狗。

男：我明。

【停頓】

男：你點培養你隻狗㗎？佢識自己去廁所嗎？

【停頓】

女：乜你慣咗咁溝女㗎？

男：……

女：同你傾計好奇怪 一

男：Sorry 一

女：唔使 sor sor sor 㗎一

男：Sorry 一

女：OK stop. 你……記唔記得……你係咪有啲嘢想同我講？

男：嗯？

女：即係……唔係關於仔呀寵物呀嗰啲。

男：係……

女：你記唔記得……

【少女拿出手機查看】

女：……我哋係喺微信度傾過啲咩？

男：記得，好多添，我哋傾過好多嘢先約出嚟㗎嘛。

15

女：係吖係吖。

男：愛好啦、理想啦、啲心煩嘢啦……

女：係吖係吖。

【停頓】

男：呼，真係好，我啱先仲以為你變咗第二個人，睇嚟第一次
見 / 係有少少唔慣嘅……

女：等等。

男：咩？

女：心煩嘢呀。

男：吓？

女：繼續啦，你記得我講咗啲咩心煩嘢嘛？

男：……記得。

女：係咩吖？

男：……等錢使？

女：唔係吖。

男：唔係？

女：我要幫屋企人醫病呀。

男：所以……呢？

女：你話過……想幫我嘛。

男：……係，係咩？

女：係㗎。

男：噢。

女：咁……你宜家……

男：吓？

【少女微笑】

16

女：放心⋯⋯

男：咩？

女：我識做嘅。

男：做⋯⋯咩呀？

女：扑嘢。

【靜默】

男：⋯⋯Sorry.

女：⋯⋯

男：我哋係咪有啲咩⋯⋯誤會？

女：吓？

男：我哋係微信度傾咗咁耐，我好似冇印象⋯⋯

女：⋯⋯

男：我諗住⋯⋯以為我哋係有⋯⋯

女：咩？

男：共識。

女：⋯⋯係吖。

男：或者講係投契喇，係咪？

女：⋯⋯係。

男：你記唔記得，我⋯⋯哋最尾話，得閒嘅話上嚟坐下⋯⋯

女：係吖。

男：飲杯嘢⋯⋯

女：係吖。

男：傾下計⋯⋯

女：係吖。

【停頓】

女：然後？

男：然後⋯⋯咩然後？

女：冇然後你咁夜嗌我上嚟做咩？

男：傾計啊嘛。

女：傾計？我咁靚你叫我上嚟傾計？

男：犯法㗎？

女：然後呢？

男：⋯⋯

女：冇然後？

男：⋯⋯

女：你想我信你⋯⋯冇然後？

【男子拿出手機】

男：唔係唔係，咁喇或者我哋可以開返個微信 check 返個
　　record——

女：我‧收‧錢‧㗎！

【停頓】

女：我唔係嚟同你玩 one night stand 㗎。

【停頓】

女：明解？

【沉默】

男：咁⋯⋯你係咪算做緊⋯⋯援交？

【停頓】

女：你鍾意點嗌都好。

男：其實我冇諗過——

女：扮嘢呀？

【停頓】

女：全世界都係咁做㗎喇，你同我講你唔知？

【沉默】

男：Sorry.

女：……

男：睇嚟真係誤會。

女：……

男：唔好意思阻你咁耐。

女：……

男：你……你可以走喇。

女：你玩嘢呀？

【沉默】

【少女背起手袋走到門邊】

【男子神情猶豫，深吸了一口氣】

男：唔係，你返嚟先……

女：……

男：Sorry，我諗咗諗……

【少女看著他】

男：你都係返嚟先……返嚟坐吖，please.

【少女慢慢地回到沙發，坐下】

男：唔好意思。

【少女打開手機】

女：嗱，我收開呢個數。

【少女打出數字給男子看】

女：兩個鐘之後我仲有嘢做。

男：好夜喇喎。

女：So？

男：去做咩？

【少女坐到男子身旁，將手放在他的腿上】

女：一陣你咪知囉⋯⋯

【少女向男子伸手，示意付錢】

男：我哋之前傾開好多⋯⋯

女：嗯哼？

男：你⋯⋯咩 feel 都冇？

女：你想要咩 feel？

男：我⋯⋯

女：嗯哼？

男：我真係當你係 friend 㗎⋯⋯

女：我唔係⋯⋯咩？

男：咁喇，不如我哋傾多陣計瞭解多啲對方先好唔好？

【停頓】

女：屌！冇錢俾早響啦！

【少女起身欲離去】

【男子起身從錢包抽出一千元港幣】

男：呢度一千，仲有一千，遲啲俾。

【停頓】

男：坐吖。

【女方坐下】

女：你真係好特別呀。

【停頓】

男：係嘞，你啱先講咩話？

女：你真係 / 好……

男：唔係唔係，之前嗰句。

女：冇錢俾 / 早響……

男：唔係唔係唔係，仲差個字。

女：（吸了口氣）……

男：由宜家開始我唔想聽到呢個字，OK？

【靜默】

【男子為少女倒了一碗 Vodka】

男：飲啦。

【停頓】

【少女抿了一口】

【沉默】

【少女起身，環視四周】

女：你呢處……都 OK 吖，幾企理吖。

男：多謝。

女：住咗幾耐？

男：都……幾耐下喇 —

女：租㗎？

男：梗係啦。

女：但出邊好難頂，有陣除嘅。

男：噢，有 BB 屙尿。

女：吓？

男：我講緊啲狗。

女：哦……

男：俾我見到一定執件返嚟打邊爐。

【停頓】

女：咁憎狗仲住響度？

男：平囉。

女：係囉，下面咁嘅環境益晒你啦。

【停頓】

女：你返咩工㗎？

男：……失業。

【沉默】

【少女看到冰箱上有一座未完成的模型，是一座樓，裡邊有隻河馬公仔。模型旁邊擺放著一個魔方】

女：隻河馬好憨鳩。

男：……

女：同你好似。

男：邊窟？

女：對矇眼。

男：哦。

女：你鍾意砌模型？

【少女走近觀察模型】

男：咩都砌……

女：咦，未砌完㗎喎。

男：砌牌啦、砌扭計骰啦……

女：紙㗎喎，咁特別嘅？

男：嗥！呢隻扭計骰，用咗我成個月先砌好，成個月呀頂。

【男子拿下魔方給少女】

22

【停頓】

【少女接過魔方】

女：你失業？

男：係。

【少女把魔方打亂，若無其事地塞回男子手裡】

女：咁咪有嘢做囉。

【少女將模型端下來】

男：（嚴肅地）唔——好——亂——郁。

女：送俾邊個㗎？

男：……

女：靚女嚟㗎？

男：……

女：北姑？

男：……

女：細路女？

男：……

女：初戀情人？

男：……

女：講兩句啦好無？

男：……

女：我好配合㗎喇已經。

男：……

女：唔開心？

男：……

女：做咩唔開心？

男：……

女：有咩唔開心講俾姐姐聽下？

男：不如等我問返你吖……

女：問吖。

男：點解揀呢行呢你？

【停頓】

女：BB 病咗。

【第一場完】

第二場 奇境

第二場　奇境

【少年獨自一人】

少年：我從未意識到我會係今日嘅自己，我好奇嘅係，人係點樣一步步咁慢慢變化，或者講，進化？人類由猿人開始，經歷咗咁鬼耐嘅演變，我好奇，作為呢條長河中嘅一滴，我完成咗啲咩呢？就好似你嗌髮型師剪個光頭，你究竟由邊一刀開始可以稱之為真正嘅光頭仔。我居然一直思考緊呢個咁憨鳩嘅問題，我諗，可能因為我，我呢個人，不知不覺地，似乎起緊啲變化。

【敘述者轉為男子】

男：嗰日，我行經一條巷仔，一條深不見底嘅巷仔，我對任何深不見底嘅事物都十分之感興趣，於是乎我捐咗入去，爬咗上一條星光熠熠、五彩斑爛嘅樓度，香甜嘅氣息撲面而嚟，熟悉，又神秘。

一個鐘之後，我坐咗喺佢嘅床邊，左手輕輕撫摸佢嘅長髮，右手拉住佢隻手，我話：「我係時候要走嘞。」我錫咗佢一啖，留低咗冚把，同埋幾舊水。

【第二場完】

26

第三場 逃難

第三場　逃難

時間：數年前，夏天的某個下午。
地點：李可的家中。
人物：李可、秦薈。

【在李可的家裡，門被打開，秦薈進門把高跟鞋踢在一邊，倒在沙發上，李可提著行李箱，頭夾著手機，蹣跚地走進來，邊說話邊關上門】

可：（超速地）……嗱，陳太，老實講我淨係負責補習嘅，其他問題我哋唔處理嘅，咁喇，我可以同你傾耐少少，遲啲從你個女嘅補習時間度扣番。一句講曬，你個女成績差係因為佢唔想讀你哋係都要逼佢讀你哋越逼佢佢越唔想讀簡單嚟講佢讀傻咗。（停頓）另外其實我都做開保險嘅，如果你擔心改制會影響你個女升學，我誠意推介你買我哋呢個末代文憑保險……聽唔明？講普通話？好……

【李可深吸一口氣】

可：（國）Linda 讀 "傻——" 了，（停頓）她需要一份保險。

【停頓】

可：（國）Linda 是你個女，你個女的英文名叫 Linda。陳太，不好意思，我老細叫我，遲點再聊。

【李可關掉電話，深呼吸】

可：Sorry。

【李可放好行李箱，看著秦薈】

可：想飲啲咩？

【停頓】

可：水？

【停頓】

可：汽水？

【停頓】

可：檸檬水？

【停頓】

可：今晚你住喺度喇。

薑：……

可：你有冇帶毛巾？幫你拎出嚟？

薑：……

【李可坐到沙發扶手上，撫著她的頭】

可：去沖涼先，嗯？

薑：我好劫……真係好劫……

【沉默】

薑：返大陸嘅尾班車係咪八點？

可：係。

【秦薑看了看手錶】

薑：好混亂，我個頭就嚟爆嘞。

【沉默】

薑：我嘅一個好姊妹呃我嚟呢處，呵好姊妹好姊妹，媽臭閪，自己就走咗去第度搵大錢，我困喺間套房度四日四夜了，日日就對住四堵牆，又濕又暗，又唔俾出門，好似坐監咁。今日天文臺個老細同我話要計房錢，仲有飯錢，屌，我喺度做撚左四日四夜先夠車錢返，（國）媽的當本小姐傻逼啊？

可：所以你想返去？

29

薈：我想即走添啊，本小姐一個人拖住咁大個喼由走火通道拖
　　咗十四層樓偷走出嚟㗎。（國）我操你媽香港的路走來走
　　去一模一樣，我都快瘋了，搞到我大白天的帶著個大濃妝
　　到處去嚇人。

【停頓】

薈：我淨係得你電話 —

可：隨叫隨到。

薈：如果你敢呃我你就死梗。

【沉默】

薈：你係老師？

可：呵，兼職啫，好少見？

薈：我識好多個老師。

【停頓】

可：要唔要沖涼？

薈：我好肚餓。

可：咁你擺低啲嘢響度，我哋落去食。

薈：食咩？咖喱牛肉？

可：呵。

薈：真係唔知香港地有咩咁好，啲嘢難食到死，啲人就係死都
　　要湧埋入嚟。

可：嚟，我帶你去食啲好嘢。

【停頓】

可：你未行過維港㗎嘛？我哋食完去果邊睇睇，好靚㗎 —

薈：唔去。

可：嚟香港唔睇維港等於白行㗎嘞喎。

30

薹：夜晚仲要趕車。

可：嚟得切㗎。

薹：你夠膽呃我你就死硬。

【停頓】

薹：個咩咩港 —

可：維港，維多利亞港 —

薹：有咩咁好睇？

可：嗰度有海啦，公園啦，仲有條星光大道，好多明星仲喺嗰
　　處打咗手印添。

薹：咩明星？

可：好多喎。

薹：有冇周星馳？

可：梗係有啦。

薹：我鍾意周星馳！有冇劉德華？

可：梗係有啦。

薹：我鍾意劉德華！有冇曾志偉？

可：梗係有啦。

薹：佢係咪真係好撚矮？

可：係。

薹：劉德華真係好撚型？

可：係。

【秦薹打著哈欠伸懶腰，無意將手伸向身後的玻璃窗】

薹：（半撒嬌地）仲有啲咩啫……

【秦薹回頭望見窗上有一隻壁虎，跳了起來】

薹：哇！癡線㗎？！

可：你跳得好高。

薈：咩嚟㗎？！

可：檐蛇。

薈：燒燶咗咁嘅？！

可：曬燶咗。

薈：癲線！唔同你玩喇。

【秦薈穿鞋】

可：去邊？

薈：睇周星馳！

【第三場完】

第四場 竹馬

第四場　竹馬

時間：與上場同一日傍晚。
地點：維港附近的一個兒童樂園。
人物：同上。

可：哇！你睇你個樣。

薑：好樣衰，刪左佢。

可：呵呵，好鄉下。

薑：刪咗佢。

可：真係好撚鄉下。

薑：刪呀。

可：哇！你睇吓呢張，你對手真係好撚死大。

薑：喏先個手印真係曾志偉嘅？

可：係呀。

薑：好撚 cute 呀佢對手！

可：人地唔夠高啫。

薑：好 cute 呀！我真係諗唔到佢咁矮㗎，好矮呀，真係好撚矮呀佢！佢阿媽做乜生到佢咁撚死矮㗎！哈哈哈！

可：飲唔飲嘢呀？

【李可站在自助販賣機前，拍八達通卻沒有反應】

可：咦，部機好似壞壞咃。

【李可拍了拍機器】

薑：唉，你有睇過周星馳嘅電影咩？佢頭一次嚟香港買水嗰部哩。

可：右，示範下。

薆：「呀 Sir 呀 Sir，第一次嚟香港，俾啲面醒我兩啖水啦。」

【靜默】

【機器落下兩支檸檬茶】

薆：嚀。

【停頓】

薆：我要去玩前面個公園仔！

可：你識唔識呢支檸檬茶呀？

薆：唔識。

可：你細細個肯定睇過隻廣告，「咦，乜咁啱嘅？」。

薆：噢！唔識喎。

可：咁你點知周星馳㗎？

薆：土豆網。

【停頓】

薆：哇，我要玩嗰隻鞦韆！喂屄，個細路咁撚快手嘅？

可：嚟玩呢個呀，呢隻馬好得意㗎。

【李可騎上彈簧馬】

可：喳！喳！

薆：……

可：喳！嚟喇！你騎嗰隻，超有 feel。

薆：呵，好撚青山！

可：嚟喇！

薆：真係好撚青山！

可：快啲！嚟追我！

薆：呵呵呵呵！

【秦薑騎上彈簧馬】

薑：喳！喳！

【兩人互相追逐，興致勃勃】

【忽地，一切事物似乎放慢了十倍，兩人像在一塊巨大啫喱中奔跑】

可：喂——！

薑：喳！

可：喂——！

薑：喳！

可：姑娘——！

薑：吓——？

可：你係邊度人呀——！

薑：你唔使知㗎——！喳——！

可：喳——！點解呀——！

薑：我自己都唔知呀——！

可：等我幫吓你喇——！

薑：你幫唔到㗎喳——！喳——！

可：喳——！你停低先啦——！

薑：我停唔到呀——！

可：你要去邊呀——！

薑：返去呀——！

可：返邊呀——！

薑：我都唔知呀——！喳——！

可：喳——！宜家黃昏喇，抖下喇——！

薑：抖唔到呀——！

可：我隻馬就仆死喇——！

薑：幫唔到你喇——！

【秦薑縱身一跳，躍進一條河流】

【這條河流仿佛是啫喱做的】

可：喂——！

【李可尾隨其後】

可：你要游去邊呀——！

薑：返去呀——！

可：錯晒喇——！

薑：由得佢啦——！

可：對面係港島呀——！

薑：咁劃平佢啦——！

可：唔好游喇——！

薑：好自由呀——！

可：再游就去咗太平洋喇——！

薑：好太平呀——！

可：宜家天都黑晒喇——！

薑：黑啲好呀，睇得清啲呀——！

可：游唔返嚟喇——！

薑：返到嚟——！地球圓嚟嘛——！

【秦薑爬上新大陸，一路狂奔】

【這似乎是一座啫喱做的新大陸】

【李可尾隨】

【兩人喘著氣，一切回到了正常的速度】

可：喂！你唔仆嘅咩！

薈：堅持住呀！

可：堅持咩呀！

薈：唔好放棄呀！

可：放棄咩呀！

薈：好快到㗎喇！

可：到邊呀？

薈：好快完㗎喇！

可：完咩呀？

薈：你見唔見到呀？！

可：見咩呀？

薈：流星呀！

可：邊度呀？

薈：拖住條尾呀！

可：邊有呀！

薈：斷咗尾嘅流星呀！

可：飛機嚟㗎嘛！

薈：追啦！

可：追？

薈：佢曉飛呀！

可：佢唔會停㗎！

薈：佢會一直飛嗎？！

可：宜家就快天光㗎喇！

薈：唔好呀！

可：就嚟天光喇！

薈：我唔要呀！

可：天光喇！

薑：追喇！再唔追！呢世都趕唔切㗎喇！

【李可停下腳步】

【第四場完】

第五場 白癡

第五場　白癡

時間：同一天，晚上八點。
地點：李可家中。
人物：同上。

【緊接上一場】
【鐵閘被拉開，秦薑急速走向行李箱】
薑：一日都係你，仆街搞到我就嚟趕唔切。
【李可關上門，倚靠在門口】
可：實遲㗎嘞 ─
薑：我理撚得你 ─
可：遲硬㗎嘞 ─
薑：我一定要即刻離開呢度。
【秦薑拉起行李箱走到門口，李可一把抓住她的手】
可：今晚留低陪我，OK？
薑：我要返屋企。
【沉默】
【李可鬆手】
可：走啦走啦，我都唔鍾意勉強……
【沉默】
【秦薑放下行李，打算給他一個擁抱】
【李可將她擁入懷中，吻她】
薑：玩嘢呀？
可：點嘛？

【停頓】

蕓：玩嘢呀？

可：點嘛？

蕓：你夠膽呃我你就死梗 —

可：咁你上嚟做咩？—

蕓：攞唸。

可：然後呢？

蕓：走。

可：咁宜家呢？

【秦蕓掙扎，李可不放】

蕓：放手。

【秦蕓掙扎，李可不放】

蕓：放開我，仲老師添。

【秦蕓掙扎，李可不放】

蕓：你啲男人全部都係仆街！—

可：啱吖。

蕓：（國）全他媽混蛋！—

可：係吖。

蕓：（國）操蛋！—

可：係吖。

蕓：（國）雞巴蛋！—

可：咩話？

【李可鬆開手，兩人對視】

蕓：想點？

【李可吻她】

【秦薈推開】

薈：鍾意你點算先？

【停頓】

可：你夠膽嚟我咪夠膽受囉。

【停頓】

薈：（國）騙子。

可：點嘛？

薈：當我白癡呀？

【李可吻她】

【秦薈推開，指著他鼻子】

薈：你後悔一世。

【李可吻她】

【秦薈推開，繼續指著他鼻子】

薈：話你知我唔同第啲女人，我會黐到你實一實，（國）就算
　　你逃到天涯海角化了灰我都把你挖出來！

【停頓】

薈：驚呀？

可：呵。

薈：我話你聽，你夠膽……

【李可將秦薈強行拖到床上】

【他們在床上廝打了一陣】

【李可要脫她的衣服】

【秦薈給了李可一記耳光】

【停頓】

【李可笑了笑】

【秦薈給了他又一記耳光】

【李可只管埋下頭去,秦薈逐漸停止反抗】

【李可要脫她的衣服】

【秦薈伸手關掉床頭燈】

【李可打開】

【秦薈又關掉】

可:搞咩?

薈:就咁喇。

可:怕醜呀?

薈:我鍾意咁。

【李可繼續】

【第五場完】

第六場 **我的名字**

第六場　我的名字

時間：同一天深夜。
地點：李可家。
人物：同上。

【一片凌亂的臥室】
【李可斜躺在床上，閉著眼，喘著氣】
【秦薈穿著李可的 T 恤站在茶几旁，仍舊活力十足】
【她倒了杯水，咕嚕咕嚕地喝下】
【她環視了一下李可的房間】
【又倒了一杯，遞給李可】
薈：你唔噴香水嘅？
可：吓？
薈：點解你讀過書都唔噴香水？
可：咩話？
薈：你下次唔噴香水唔好出嚟見我。
可：吓？
薈：有右煙？
【李可拿出煙和火機，李可為秦薈點煙】
可：仲以為你唔食添。
薈：點解今日唔見你食煙？
可：因為……因為打茄輪陣味會好怪 ─
薈：你一早諗住同我打茄輪？
可：有咩問題？

薑：哼。

【沉默】

【薑從手袋裡拿出一隻河馬公仔】

薑：似唔似？

可：咩？

薑：你。

可：我？邊窟？我都冇肚腩。

薑：憨鳩，你哋一樣咁憨鳩。

可：吓？

薑：仲有。

可：咩？

薑：鹹濕。

可：睇唔出喎。

薑：同你一樣眼細細。

可：吓？

薑：俾你。

【停頓】

薑：整唔見就閪鳩你。

【李可拿起端詳】

薑：噂，我覺得你應該將佢擺響……

【秦薑拿起河馬，放在冰箱上的別墅模型內】

薑：呢度。

【停頓】

薑：喵晒，咁佢以後就有地方住喇。

【秦薑坐到李可身邊】

【李可摘下她手中的煙】

可：啲煙食剩三分之一就唔好食嘞。

【停頓】

可：不如講吓你。

薈：我？

可：關於你啲嘢。

薈：點解？

可：瞭解下。

薈：做咩無啦啦瞭解我？

可：想咯，你嗌咩名都未知。

薈：唔係講過咩？—

可：法拉利？你唔好「（國）開玩笑」啦。

薈：個名唔好咩？

可：冇人個名嗌法拉利㗎。

薈：法拉利咩嚟㗎？

【停頓】

可：車。

薈：好貴㗎？

可：名車，唔係是但邊個都揸到㗎。

薈：哇，咁你宜家咪好撚幸福。

可：呵。

【李可看著她】

可：你好靚。

薈：我知呀。

可：呵。

薈：好明顯喇嘛，使唔使講到出晒面呀。

可：呵。

【停頓】

薈：我叫阿薈。

可：雲？邊朵雲呀？

薈：我識寫㗎，有冇筆？我寫俾你吖。

【李可遞給秦薈一張小紙條和筆】

薈：好似係咁，「薈」，係咪？

可：係……我唔係好確定。

薈：下？你係咪老師嚟㗎？

可：……呢個係簡體—

薈：哎呀好肉酸呀。

可：你……唔識寫字㗎咩？

薈：……我冇讀過書。

【停頓】

可：嘩！你真好彩，咁我以後同你補習喇。

薈：啤！

可：嗱，我將你個名同埋隻河馬一齊黐埋響度。

薈：想點嘛？

可：咁我以後咪可以經常見到你囉。

【李可將小紙條貼在河馬的額頭上】

【停頓】

薈：呵呵。

可：笑咩？

薈：好似殭屍。

【停頓】

薑：河馬殭屍。

【停頓】

薑：殭屍河馬。

【停頓】

薑：呵呵。

【停頓】

可：點解你冇讀書嘅？

【沉默】

薑：因為我係個孤兒。

【第六場完】

第七場 紅燭

第七場　紅燭

時間：同上。
地點：同上。
人物：秦薹。

【緊接上一場】
【秦薹一人】

薹：（國）我是個孤兒，養父養母從小就告訴我說長大了要嫁
給他們兒子。有天半夜哥哥要吃荷包蛋，我點了一支紅色
蠟燭進了廚房，剛熱鍋，他就進來了，從背後靠近我，他
的呼吸帶著刺鼻的酒氣直往我耳裡鑽。「來嘛，老婆」，
他邊說，邊將我推倒在地。我呆在那，不動，鈕扣解開了，
忽地上半身著了火一樣疼，紅色的液體一滴、兩滴……像
一支一支的箭，刺穿我的脖子、乳房、小腹……呵，這是
什麼呢？我也不懂，所以我把眼睛閉上……你大概認為我
很害怕，是的，剛開始的時候是的，但當你的世界只有洗
衣做飯砍柴餵豬的時候，你就知道顫抖的快感是有多寶
貴。人一開始總是害怕的，但只要克服了自己，你就會懂
得這害怕裡面有許多別人不知道的好處。哥哥去外省唸書
後，家裡的蠟燭更是用得飛快，我每晚都要，忽明忽暗的
火光，像夢一樣，溫暖的液體飛向我的胸口，迅速凝固，
緊貼著我，包容著我。呵，這是興奮！這就是快樂……忽
地我怕！我好怕會永遠被綁在這。於是……我跑了出來。
（粵）我困喺嗰處十幾年居然走咗出嚟，村外邊原來仲有
鎮，鎮出邊原來仲有城市，北京，上海，深圳，香港。我
去工廠，去骨場，咩都做，咩都肯做，好多啊，人哋唔做
嗰啲我做晒。

【第七場完】

54

第八場 習慣

第八場　習慣

時間：回到第一場。
地點：男子家中。
人物：男子、少女。

【男子與少女在抽煙，兩人已喝至微醺】
【男子不停玩著手中的魔方】
女：好熱呀。
男：個天悶悶哋。
女：係你啲 Vodka 呀。
【少女脱下外套】
男：可能會落雨。
女：開窗吖唔該。
【男子拉開窗簾，打開窗】
女：你係補習老師？
男：曾經啦。
女：仲做埋保險？
男：係呀。
女：你咩都做嘅。
男：係呀，Starbucks 啦，PCCW 啦，MTR 啦，送水啦……
女：做咩失業呀？
男：……
女：你點交租呀？
男：……

女：噢，你攞 —

男：綜援啊嘛。

女：……

男：我而家攞晒㗎。

女：而家？噢你簽 —

男：「衰仔紙」吖嘛。

女：……

男：食好住好瞓好，生活質素超級好。

女：……

男：嚟，食餅吖，唔使錢㗎。

【少女看了看錶】

男：你哋呢行係咪好大機會上岸㗎 —

女：邊行呀？

男：援交。

【停頓】

女：你好似好瞭解咁喎。

男：見過咁囉。

女：你唔好話我聽秦蓁俾人包咗喎。

男：你覺得會？

女：我點知啫。

男：你覺得呢？

女：總之我唔需要。

【停頓】

男：你真係為咗醫你隻狗？

女：係。

男：……

女：好出奇咩？

男：……

女：為咗 BB 我做咩都制。

男：……

女：你唔會明㗎嘞。

男：我細嗰陣收養過一隻狗。

女：……

男：有次我喺橋底玩，發現喺河邊有個紙皮盒漂吓漂吓，仲傳
　　嚟啲奇怪嘅聲，我行近佢，原來有隻狗仔四腳朝天瞓喺入
　　面，一見到我就細細聲叫，好似識笑咁，好鬼得意。然後
　　我靜靜雞帶咗佢返屋企，餵佢食咗啲保濟丸，然後收埋響
　　床底。

女：你都幾有愛心 —

男：第朝佢死咗。

女：……

男：我唔知點處理條屍，就由佢擺喺床底先。冇幾日就嘔臭晒，
　　啲烏蠅飛晒入房，後尾仲俾老豆打鑊金。

女：好慘呀……你係咪好傷心？

男：我好後悔。

女：你冇錯吖。

【停頓】

男：其實我之前有同你講過少少。

女：我知呀。

男：你知？

女：我記得吖，你仲話有時唔知點同其他人相處啊嘛。

58

男：係。

女：所以我宜家咪喺度幫你囉。

【停頓】

男：其實你真係冇當過我⋯⋯（係 friend ？）

女：⋯⋯

男：你真係一啲都唔記得⋯⋯

女：嗯？

男：⋯⋯

【男子放下魔方，拿起捲煙器走到窗邊捲煙】

男：秦薑後尾行咗去佢阿哥公司附近搵嘢做。

女：吓？做咩行埋去呀佢？

【少女看了看錶】

男：幾靚喎隻錶，你好鍾意戴錶？

【停頓】

女：算係啦—

男：借我睇睇？

【少女取下，遞給男子】

【男子接過手錶，帶在手上，繼續捲煙】

女：秦薑做乜去搵佢阿哥呀？

男：我冇咁講過喎。

女：咁佢做乜走埋去佢阿哥附近？

男：去搵佢。

【停頓】

女：OK，你唔想傾就算啦。

【少女抬手看錶，發現錶不在】

女：……

【停頓】

女：如果冇其他嘢我走㗎喇。

男：秦薈去照顧佢阿哥。

女：佢做乜仲行埋去？

【停頓】

女：咩事呀佢？

【停頓】

【少女抬起手，發現沒錶，於是捋了捋頭髮】

【少女抬頭，發現男子正注視著她】

男：嗱，錢你就收咗，我宜家有個要求……

【男子拿起魔方丟給少女】

男：幫我砌返佢吖，唔該。

【停頓】

【少女擺弄魔方】

【傳來雨點打落在窗戶的聲音】

【雨聲漸強】

【男子關上窗，注視著窗外，或是窗上的壁虎】

女：然後呢？

男：佢走唔甩。

女：走唔甩？點解走唔甩？

男：俾個男人黐實咗。

女：個男人做咗啲咩？

男：佢洗晒佢啲錢。

女：佢俾錢佢？

60

【男子點了一支捲煙,吸了一口】

女:佢點解俾錢佢?

【停頓】

女:點解呀?

【男子將手中點燃的煙遞給少女】

【第八場完】

第九場　**我的身體**

第九場　我的身體

時間：數年前的某個晚上。

地點：東莞市長安鎮某家足浴中心的一間客房內。

人物：李可、秦薈。

【緊接上一場】

【床上，光線昏暗，秦薈穿著暴露的工作服，在給李可按摩】

可：點解呀？

【秦薈沒有理會】

【隱隱約約，門外不斷傳來服務生爽朗的吆喝，伴隨著女孩們的應答】

【外：「歡迎光臨樓上老闆一位——！」】

【秦薈將李可翻過來】

薈：（國）放鬆。

【秦薈「咔、咔」兩下快速地扭動了李可的頭，動作純熟】

薈：（國）好了。

【秦薈撕開安全套】

薈：（國）脫。

【李可抓住秦薈的手】

可：你有冇聽我講嘢？點解吖？

【外：「大哥請帶齊您的隨身物品歡迎下次光臨謝謝——！」】

【秦薈想掙脫，李可緊緊不放】

薈：（國）放開！

可：點解？

【停頓】

蕓：應該我問你。

【停頓】

蕓：點解仲嚟搵我？

【李可鬆手】

【秦蕓走至窗邊點了一支煙】

蕓：答我呀。

可：⋯⋯

蕓：我冇幾多時間㗎咋。

【外：「三十八號！三十八號準備下鐘！」】

蕓：（大聲地，國）好！等一下！

【停頓】

蕓：你鍾意響度玩冇問題，但點解要點我？

可：⋯⋯

蕓：你究竟想點？

可：見下你，傾兩句 ─

蕓：然後？

【停頓】

蕓：有冇然後？

【停頓】

蕓：然後你俾錢我。

【停頓】

蕓：然後我去隔離房繼續做。

【停頓】

蕓：做天光。

【停頓】

薈：然後你返香港。

【停頓】

薈：係咪？

可：你可以過嚟㗎─

薈：唔・去。

可：你嚟香港一樣做㗎。

【秦薈轉過身，注視著他】

薈：（國）我這輩子再也不要去香港那個鬼地方。聽清楚了嗎？

可：你好憎我咩宜家？

薈：（國）是的，我從來從來沒這麼討厭過一個人。

可：我做啲咩令你咁反感？

薈：（國）身份證還給我！

可：……

薈：（國）聽到沒有？你知道內地辦證有多難嗎？─

可：我講過，嚟香港搵我就俾返你─

薈：（國）你知道我現在每天擔驚受怕的嗎？走在大街上看見
　　警察就不停地抖！

可：點解仲要嚟搵你阿哥吖？

薈：（國）OK，那身份證老娘不要了，還有，那麼喜歡拿我的
　　東西是吧……

【秦薈從手袋裡拿出通行證扔在地上】

薈：（國）給！港澳通行證！按摩免費送的！

可：我唔會要㗎。

薈：（國）你看到這房間了嗎？我可以在這裡蹦在這裡跑在這

裡打側手翻！老娘還可以抽煙！打開這扇大窗還可以往外跳還可以大叫：啊──！！！還可以完全聽懂別人在說什麼不會被騙！

可：（國）我家也能抽煙 ─

薈：（忽地溫柔）（國）我‧可‧以‧永‧遠‧留‧在‧你‧家‧嗎？

【沉默】

薈：我有 BB 嘞。

【停頓】

【李可看了一眼她手中的煙】

可：你打算點？

薈：生。

可：玩嘢？

【停頓】

可：你係咪以為咁樣就可以綁住你阿哥／可以有個人陪你過世吖？

薈：（快速地）我鍾意細路你明唔明吖？（國）我想有個家我想有個屬於自己的家！

【沉默】

薈：你呢？

可：……

薈：你……明白你做緊咩嗎？

可：……

薈：你……話過我好靚㗎，係咪？

可：……

薈：但你一直都覺得我未睇夠未睇透，係咪？

可：……

蕓：你一直都好好奇，點解我次次都一定要熄燈，係嗎？

可：……

【秦蕓脱下衣服，一手拿著衣服，同時注視著李可】

【「嗒」一聲，秦蕓伸手打開了燈】

【她的腰、腹、背似乎佈滿了傷痕】

【較長沉默】

蕓：（國）這就是我。

可：……

蕓：（國）沒辦法改變的我。

可：……

蕓：（國）看清楚了嗎？

可：……

蕓：（國）還有什麼想説嗎？

【第九場完】

第十場 **夜遊**

第十場　夜遊

【少年一人】

少年：好奇係一種人類嘅優點，但太好奇，有時係會死人㗎。

【停頓】

少年：我係一個普通人，有個普通嘅屋企，我一直普通地認為呢個係一個普通嘅世界，誠實守信、潔身自好、講好普通話……呢啲亦都係我一直嚮往嘅普通生活。我原本可以好普通好平靜好平常咁度過我嘅青春。

【停頓】

少年：但我太好奇嘞……

【敘述者轉為男子】

【男子一人】

男：嗰一年冬，新年前嘅最後一晚，我行咗上蘭桂坊想飲兩杯，好多人喺呢處倒數，好熱鬧，其實如果要計呢個世上最有趣嘅事，倒數絕對係無聊到反艇。我都係無聊人，所以都出現喺呢處，期待著零點嗰刻有個鬼妹飛撲埋嚟係咁咀我。結果我買唔到酒，喺蘭桂坊嘅人海之中塞咗半個鐘先出嚟。我沿著條電車路一路散步行到去筲箕灣，我一路行一路諗，人生真係好撚無聊。積極，自信，一份穩定嘅人工，要有愛心，孝順屋企人，搵個靠得住嘅女人，買樓，生仔，湊大佬……我經已可以預計到我嘅一切，但我心入邊有把聲話我知佢好唔爽，我唔知係咩，太 normal 喇太 normal 喇，我需要一啲……唔尋常嘅……刺激，冇錯嘞，係刺激，冒險，我好好奇，我究竟仲有冇得變，作為一個所謂嘅良好青年，我究竟仲可以變成點…我真係好好奇，好好奇，好奇到不得了。

於是乎……

【第十場完】

第十一場　疑問

第十一場　疑問

時間：多年前，新年第一天的凌晨。

地點：一座舊唐樓

人物：少年、汪靜。

【傳來輕哼的歌聲】

【汪靜，保持上一場秦薑的位置和姿勢】

【「嗒」一聲，她打開了燈，定住，看了看監控】

【汪靜穿上衣服，不小心觸碰到痛處，呻吟了一下】

【少年在門外來回躊躇】

【忽地，門打開，少年受到驚嚇，汪靜注視著他】

【停頓】

靜：進來吧。

【停頓】

【少年入，環顧四周】

少年：哇！咩嚟㗎？

靜：C‧C‧T‧V。

少年：你睇到我㗎？

靜：對呀，你被拍下了。

【停頓】

少年：你識聽廣東話㗎喎。

靜：O‧K‧吧。

【停頓】

少年：成三點幾都仲唔休息？

靜：等·你·啊。

【汪靜開始幫少年脫衣服。】

少年：做咩？

靜：你來這不知道要幹嘛的嗎？

少年：⋯⋯

靜：沖個涼先吧，呀你自己脫好了。

少年：哇！好大隻蜥蜴呀！

靜：怎麼？

【少年指著天花板】

靜：噢，那是小白。

少年：小白？你居然同隻蜥蜴起咗個名？

靜：它是一隻壁虎 —

少年：檐蛇？

靜：對對對，你們是這麼叫的。

少年：咁肥嘅檐蛇？

靜：因為它幫我吃了好多蚊子。對吧小白？

少年：整走佢。

【汪靜沒有理會，開始脫衣服】

少年：做咩？

靜：又問？沖涼啊。

少年：噢。

靜：你不喜歡？

少年：唔係呀。

【停頓】

靜：快脫！

少年：可唔可以請佢迴避吓？

【汪靜拿出一支網兜，遞給少年】

靜：男人，上。

【少年猶豫了一會兒，跳上床】

【汪靜靠在牆邊】

【少年嘗試捉壁虎，他一舉起手壁虎便快速地爬動】

靜：傷了它你要賠錢噢。

【少年的目光隨著壁虎唰唰地快速轉動，繞了一圈，最後轉過身來落在汪靜頭上】

【汪靜雙手拍了兩下，壁虎溜進衣櫃】

少年：……入咗衣櫃。

靜：OK 了嗎？

【汪靜脫下少年的褲子，少年急忙用網兜遮住私處】

【汪靜拉著他走進洗手間】

【傳來淋浴聲和兩人的對話】

靜：轉過來。

少年：吓？

靜：轉過來，你老屁股對著我怎麼幫你小弟洗澡？

少年：噢。

靜：皮膚還不錯。

少年：你條頸瘀咗嘅？

靜：……

少年：（驚嚇地）喂……做咩？

靜：又問！幫你洗乾淨點啊！

少年：喂……喂！

靜：嘴巴張開。

少年：做咩？

靜：含漱口水。

【少年含下漱口水】

靜：像後面，這裡，也要經常洗的，懂嗎？

【汪靜用力搓，傳來少年的呻吟】

少年：吞咗落肚。

靜：行了。向後轉！轉吶。齊步走！你在外面坐會兒。

【少年圍著浴巾出來，坐在床上】

【他拿起床頭的一塊絲綢，上面插著針線】

【浴室傳來汪靜輕哼的歌聲，《瀏陽河》】

【汪靜圍著浴巾走到床邊】

靜：好看吧？

少年：咩嚟㗎？

靜：十字繡。

【少年放下絲綢】

少年：坐。

【汪靜坐下，少年搭著她的肩膀】

少年：點稱呼吖？

靜：喲呵，變得挺快嘛。

【少年的手縮了回去】

【停頓】

靜：Benz.

少年：吓？

靜：沒聽過？

少年：Ben 屎？車名嚟㗎喎。

靜：對啊，不是誰都開得起的。

【少年一手抓住汪靜胸部】

少年：（國）那我真的好幸福噢。

【汪靜痛苦地呻吟了一下】

少年：做咩？

【汪靜搖搖頭】

靜：來，躺著，乖。

少年：噢。

【停頓】

少年：呢行做咗幾耐呀？

【停頓】

靜：幾個月吧。

【停頓】

靜：沒交女朋友嗎？

少年：有就唔使嚟搵你啦。

靜：找一個啊。

少年：好貴㗎。

靜：貴？

少年：拍拖貴呀。

靜：很少過來？

少年：第一次。

靜：噢——才這麼年輕就那麼會玩，長大還了得。

少年：我處㗎。

【停頓】

76

靜：啊？

少年：（國）我是處男。

【停頓】

【汪靜注視著他】

靜：切。

少年：（國）是真的。

【停頓】

少年：（國）你一定要信我。

【沉默】

靜：那怎麼辦？

少年：咩呀？冇咩呀。

靜：你以後別怪我。

【汪靜撕開避孕套】

少年：做咩？

靜：幫你吹啊。

【停頓】

少年：唔戴得唔得呀？（國）我好乾淨的。

【停頓】

靜：好，下不為例。

【汪靜埋下頭去】

靜：你全身發抖。

少年：可能太凍喇。

【汪靜蓋了一張毛毯在他肚子上，埋下頭去】

靜：手放開，老抓著我頭怎麼吹？

【一分鐘後】

靜：差不多了，我躺著你來？

少年：我唔係幾識……

靜：好吧，我來，做愛是一定要戴套的噢。

少年：嗯。

【汪靜拿出避孕套】

【一會兒】

【汪靜坐上去】

少年：咪住……慢啲……

靜：幹嘛？不舒服？

少年：嗯，少少。

【汪靜動】

少年：喂，咪住咪住……

【汪靜停】

少年：少少痛……

靜：頭一回是有點不習慣的。

少年：慢啲……慢啲……

【兩人靜止】

靜：軟了。

少年：Sorry.

【汪靜起身，埋下頭去】

【一分鐘後，汪靜撕開另一個避孕套，戴好】

靜：OK 了，快。

少年：慢啲！……

【汪靜加速】

少年：慢啲！

【汪靜放慢速度】

【靜默】

靜：不是吧。

少年：Sorry.

靜：你不用 sorry 的……

少年：Sorry.

靜：唉，累死老娘……

【汪靜埋下頭去】

少年：我會投入啲㗎喇。

【一會兒，汪靜抬起頭】

靜：我躺著你來，快。

少年：噢。

【少年忙了一陣】

靜：搞什麼啊？

少年：點入？

靜：給我。

少年：……

【忙了一陣】

靜：又軟了。

【少年坐在床上】

【沉默】

少年：似乎……冇乜 feel.

靜：對我啊？

少年：唔係唔係，我嘅問題……

【停頓】

靜：唉，那咋搞呢？

【沉默】

【汪靜親吻少年】

【一陣過後，汪靜再次熟練地騎了上去】

【一陣】

少年：咪住咪住……

靜：別吵，等會又軟了。

少年：唔得唔得……

【汪靜完全沒有理會】

少年：真係唔得……

靜：幹嘛！

少年：小白過緊嚟！

靜：……

少年：就嚟到我頭頂喇！

靜：再堅持一會兒！

少年：喂！喂！

【第十一場完】

80

第十二場 **故鄉的歌**

第十二場　故鄉的歌

時間：同上。

地點：同上。

人物：同上。

【床上，少年伏在汪靜身上，汪靜抱著他】

【一陣，少年翻過來。兩人神態疲憊】

【天色從一開場的昏暗，到本場結束，逐漸達到通透明亮】

靜：天要亮了。

【停頓】

靜：呼——接你一個像是接了十個。

少年：... Sorry.

靜：頭一回成績還不錯，還能再來？

【停頓】

少年：唔好難為我啦。

【停頓】

少年：個咩……小白呢？

靜：早吃飽睡了。

少年：噢，我係咪過晒鐘喇……

靜：算了，今天本來就沒什麼生意，我都繡三張十字繡了。

少年：Sorry ——

靜：説了不要再講 sorry ——

少年：Sor ...

【停頓】

【少年拿起床邊的絲綢】

少年：你繡啲咩？

靜：花。

少年：花？睇唔出。

靜：煙花。

【停頓】

少年：你鍾意繡嘢？

靜：無聊啊，這個可以消磨時間。

少年：俾邊個？

靜：我女兒。

【停頓】

靜：我可以抽煙嗎？

【少年點頭】

【汪靜點了一支煙】

靜：來一口？

【少年搖頭】

靜：來嘛，當是給你慶祝第一次。

少年：唔識喝。

靜：我教你。

【汪靜捏著煙遞到少年嘴邊】

靜：先輕輕吸一口在嘴裡……然後，像呼吸新鮮空氣一樣……

【汪靜作深呼吸狀】

【少年模仿，嗆了起來】

【汪靜笑著拍了拍他的背，遞給他一杯水】

【沉默】

靜：你真的是第一次？

少年：係。

【汪靜從床頭抽屜拿出一封利是】

靜：大吉大利。

【停頓】

少年：啊，我仲未俾你添。

靜：先拿著啦。

【停頓】

少年：Thank you！

靜：笑那麼開心？才一塊錢噢。

【沉默】

【少年想再抽一口手中的煙】

【汪靜遞過來一個煙灰缸】

靜：抽剩三分之一就可以扔掉了。

【兩人並排躺在床上望向天花板】

少年：你啱先沖涼唱緊咩呀？

靜：家鄉的歌。

少年：你鄉下邊㗎？

靜：湖南，你知道嗎？

少年：知，北方㗎嘛。

靜：我再跟你們香港人強調一遍，湖南是南方，長江以北才是
　　北方。

少年：噢。

【停頓】

少年：長江同黃河……係咩關係呀？

靜：都是水做的。

【停頓】

少年：你鄉下有咩特色呀？

靜：煙花啊，瀏陽的煙花最有名了。

少年：仲有呢？

靜：瀏陽河啊。

少年：河？靚唔靚㗎？

靜：不曉得呢，好久沒回去了。

【停頓】

靜：真的好久了。

【停頓】

靜：聽說，瀏陽河都快變臭水河了。

【停頓】

少年：做咩唔返去？

靜：回不了了。

少年：你日日踎係度唔悶嘅咩？間房一啲光線都冇。

靜：（笑）我有小白 ——

少年：你應該搣晒啲窗花，一陣我幫你 ——

靜：不行，早上太陽很猛的 ——

少年：太陽？

靜：嗯 ——

少年：呢度見到太陽？

靜：還有日出呢。

少年：咩話？

靜：日出 ——

少年：講嘢吖？

靜：你看到那棟很高的大廈麼？

少年：四周圍都係，你講邊？

靜：那兒，寫著「滙豐」兩個大字的。日出，在那兒。

少年：你有嘢嘛？

靜：那棟大廈上面有扇玻璃，可以直接把陽光反射進來。

少年：咁都得？

靜：日出的時候我整間房子像著了火一樣呢，紅通通的！

少年：呢度竟然有日出。

靜：每天五分鐘，對了，差不多就這個時候！

【房間微微地透出紅光，逐漸變亮】

【沉默良久，只聽得窗外稀稀落落的鳥鳴】

少年：你打算幾時返湖南？

靜：……

少年：你唔打算返？

靜：……

少年：做乜唔打算返呀？

靜：……

少年：唔驚屋企人等你咩？

靜：……

少年：你唔掛住屋企人咩？

【停頓】

少年：可唔可以唱多次？

靜：什麼？

少年：啱先隻歌。

【停頓】

【汪靜唱起《瀏陽河》】

靜：「瀏陽河

　　彎過了幾道彎

　　幾十里水路到湘江

　　江邊有個什麼縣哪

　　出了個什麼人

　　領導人民得解放

　　啊依呀依子喲

　　瀏陽河

　　彎過了九道彎

　　五十里水路到湘江

　　江邊有個湘潭縣哪

　　……」

【房間像似著了一片火，暖得醉人】

少年：你叫咩名？

靜：汪靜。

【第十二場完】

第十三場 **異境**

第十三場　異境

【李可，獨自一人】

可：汪靜，第一次聽呢個名，我眼前浮現嘅係一汪泉水，安安靜靜，明麗動人。

於是，我跳咗入去，潛咗落水底。

一股清涼滲入我嘅肌膚，搖曳嘅陽光掠過我嘅眼眉。我見到一架叮叮，我游咗上去，搵咗個靠窗位。架叮叮爬下爬下，爬咗去灣仔，爬下爬下，爬咗入維港，爬下爬下，爬咗去九龍。我見到喺條巷仔度有個女人深吸咗啖氣，將支未食完嘅煙掟落坑渠；啲煙圈飄去一個窗口，有個細路趴喺度，擘大對眼望著自己嘅米奇老鼠氣球飛咗上天；米奇老鼠飛去一棟大廈嘅天棚，有一座綠色嘅竹林，遠遠地，一群帶著黃色帽嘅男人擒上擒落，穿梭自如。忽地，喺我面前，一群著住橙色衫嘅魚仔飛嚟飛去，我伸手，佢哋親吻我嘅手心、手背、手指，好似蜻蜓點水。一眨眼，佢哋已經離開我飛向車窗下邊。於是，我向下望，我見到成個香港。灣仔、維港、九龍、新界……好似一張隨風搖曳嘅絲綢，上面分佈斑斑點點嘅黑色圖案，原來，係一座森林，一座似海咁深咁闊嘅森林。新年呀，新嘅一年呀，我變得完全唔識得呢個世界。

【第十三場完】

第十四場 **破冰**

第十四場　破冰

時間：回到第一場。
地點：男子家中。
人物：男子、少女。

【傳來少女的笑聲，伴隨著窗外嘩嘩的雨聲】
【少女喝得半醉，嘴裡叼著煙，手中拿著魔方在胡亂扭動】
【男子幾近完成了他的模型】

女：好慘呀！

男：……

女：好慘呀！真係好慘呀！呵呵！你啲宅男係咪個個都……唔
　　駛後悔、唔駛後悔，姐姐錫你。

【停頓】

男：呵。

女：哈，好慘。不過宜家唔同喇，多好多選擇。

男：咩唔同？

女：梗係唔同啦，我哋俾感情㗎嘛，俾力㗎！

男：呵。

女：你嗰陣時幾歲？

男：十九。

女：哈。

男：點？

女：我行先過你好多。

男：咁你呢？

92

【停頓】

女：十四。

【停頓】

女：嗌姐姐吖。

男：姐姐。

女：哈。

男：你好 pro 咁。

女：宜家為止我拍過三、四、五……七次，噢，八次！八次喇
　　已經。

男：年輕有為。

女：你真係好缺乏溫暖……

男：……

女：好慘，真係好慘，不如等姐姐溫暖下你啦？

男：十四歲係咩 feel？

【停頓】

男：十四歲有咗第一次。

女：咩 feel？

【停頓】

女：冇咩 feel 呀，想玩下就玩㗎喇下嘛……

男：拍咗幾耐？

女：……

男：一個月？

女：唔記得了。

男：一個禮拜？

女：……

男：Oh...

女：⋯⋯

【停頓】

男：汪靜有個女，叫小柔，跟佢前夫返咗去台北。後嚟我去探小柔，佢送咗呢套模型俾我，呢，可以砌出唔同花款喫。

女：呵呵呵，你同汪靜⋯⋯一直有路？

男：我幫小柔影咗幾張相，佢問我係咪見過佢媽媽。

【停頓】

男：我話，（國）「有呀，現在有種東西叫上網，很容易見面的噢。」然後，小柔攞出呢盒模型，話（國）「媽媽説等她買好一棟房子就來接我呢！你快把這個上網給她，叫她早點來！」。

女：哈哈，好得意呀佢！

男：係呀，你都快啲生返件啦！

女：哈哈，不如就今晚咯？

男：哇，你猴擒咗啲喎。

女：咁秦薈呢？

男：咩？

女：哈哈，佢有冇呀？佢有冇生呀？

男：有。

女：哈哈哈！

男：哈哈哈！

女：肯定係因為聽咗你個故仔覺得 BB 好得意喇！

男：哈哈，係呀係呀！

【男子注視著少女】

【少女倒了一碗酒】

男：你飲唔少喫嘞。

女：喂，我好飲得喫！

男：你飲左我幾舊水喫嘞。

女：我鍾意飲大就飲大！OK？哈哈！講又講吖，你講咁多係咪想扑嘢啫其實？你係咪諗住溝返件以後就可以慳返啫其實—

男：其實你係咪就係喺咁嘅情況下，右咗第一次？

【停頓】

【少女將碗砰地拍在桌上，酒水四濺】

女：好好玩呀？

男：……

女：你係咪覺得我好玩？

男：……

女：我可以陪你玩落去喫。

男：……

女：我好玩得喫。

男：你好需要有人愛—

女：多謝，我唔需要 OK？

男：你飲大喇。

女：我好清楚自己要咩。

男：你要咩？—

女：尊嚴。你呢？

男：……

女：你有冇尊嚴？

男：……

女：我可以對我啲客 say no.

男：……

女：我身上所有嘢都係自己一手一腳賺返嚟嘅。

男：……

女：你呢？

男：……

女：你憑咩用嗰種眼神同我講嘢？

男：咩眼神？—

女：我咩都唔需要，唯一需要嘅淨係尊重。你識唔識咩叫尊重？

男：我問你咩眼神啊。

女：唔好叫過幾次雞就當正自己情聖啦好唔好？你都係雞蟲嚟
　　嚟咋，你都好 cheap 㗎咋，你由一開始就係玩玩吓㗎咋。
　　你有咩資格可憐我呀？

【停頓】

男：呵，你覺得我可憐你？—

女：仲有睇唔起。

男：睇唔起？

女：一唔係你同我講咁多嘢做咩？！

男：有咩唔啱？—

女：仲要係特登講俾我聽！

男：特登？

女：仲要係講佢哋嗰陣好似直情講緊我咁！

【停頓】

男：你唔駛緊張—

96

女：我冇呀 ─

男：我唔係講緊你。

女：⋯⋯

男：我係講緊自己。

女：⋯⋯

男：係你要我講多啲自己。

女：我？

男：你嗰次喺微信度同我講㗎，你話你明我講咩㗎。

女：⋯⋯

男：我淨係想交個朋友 ─

女：朋友？你 call 援交淨係為咗交朋友？

男：我唔係 call 援交 ─

女：咁你係 call 咩？

男：我冇 call 咩。

女：咁我點解要坐喺度聽你講咁撚多嘢呀？！─

男：我俾咗錢㗎嘛 OK？！─

女：咩話？─

男：我俾咗錢㗎！你有咩資格唔滿足我呀？

女：咁就係援交囉！─

男：我講多次！唔係援交！

女：咁係咩？！

男：援交好 cheap 㗎！

【較長沉默】

女：呵，你清唔清楚自己係個咩人嚟㗎？

【少女點了一支煙】

女：你真係瞭解你嘅秦薈你嘅汪靜你嘅乜乜物物？

【停頓】

女：你真係咁懷念佢哋？咁同情佢哋？咁感激佢哋？

【停頓】

女：咁點解你咩都唔做？

男：我 —

女：點解你唔敢面對？

【停頓】

男：面對咩？

女：你嘅虛偽。

【少女忽地脫下褲子，張開雙腿，深吸了一口煙，注視著男子】

女：嚟吖。

【一片漆黑，只見隱隱發亮的煙頭】

【第十四場完】

第十五場 私奔

第十五場　私奔

時間：多年前，年三十的深夜。
地點：天水圍的一座花園內。
人物：汪靜、少年。

【一片漆黑，只見隱隱發亮的煙頭，緩緩移動】
【空曠的花園，有一條石梯往上延伸】
少年：嚟吖。
【一道火光，是汪靜點燃了火機】
靜：黑燈瞎火的這是什麼鬼地方？
少年：公園，咁嘅鐘數冇人嚟呢處喋嘞，坐吖。
【汪靜坐在石階上，少年從褲袋裡掏出東西】
【汪靜給他光】
少年：朱古力要唔要？
靜：……
少年：瑞士糖要唔要？
靜：……
少年：曲奇餅要唔要？
靜：……
少年：蛋撻？菠蘿油？
靜：……
少年：喂，我得咁多喋咋，帶出嚟好辛苦喋，唔知以為我出嚟
　　　拜神呀。
靜：哇，全揣褲袋裡了，還是熱的吧？

少年：……

【汪靜關上火機】

靜：我們有一年沒見了吧？

少年：你記得？

靜：……

少年：咁你幾個月唔接我電話？

靜：不告訴過你了嘛，他看得可緊了呢。

少年：個二世祖呀？

【停頓】

靜：大年三十的你不待家裡陪爸媽？

少年：鬼叫你咁遠行嚟天水圍話要見我一面咩。

靜：大過年的我沒地方去嘛。

少年：家下三點喇，你真係好似嗰隻小白咁，夜行動物嚟㗎。

【汪靜把煙扔掉】

靜：那你回家。

【停頓】

少年：係咪肚餓呀？—

【少年抽出一隻雞腿遞給汪靜】

靜：謝謝。

【汪靜吃了起來】

少年：小柔還好嗎？

【停頓】

【汪靜點頭】

少年：咁小白呢？點嘛？

靜：掛了。

少年：呱咗？

靜：現在還黏在窗戶上呢。

少年：點呱㗎？

靜：曬的，曬乾了，像條鹹魚一樣。

【停頓】

靜：那次你幫我把窗花撕掉，換了窗簾，有個地方膠水沒弄乾
　　淨，結果小白就黏在上面了。

少年：佢點會爬上嗰度？

靜：因為上面也黏了很多蚊子啊。

少年：……

靜：尾巴都斷開了，肯定掙扎過。

少年：你冇發現？

靜：沒有，我出去旅遊了一星期。

【停頓】

少年：同嗰二世祖？一

靜：啊，好飽呀！

【汪靜將骨頭遠遠扔出去，接著擦了擦手】

靜：開心！

【停頓】

靜：我真的好開心。

【停頓】

靜：你知道嗎？香港是個沒有煩惱的地方。

少年：係？

靜：香港是個不需要思考的地方。

少年：吓？

靜：因為香港人都跟你一樣……

少年：咩？

靜：沒腦子！哈哈！

【汪靜往高處跑了幾步，停在頂點】

少年：喂，黑麻麻小心仆親呀！

靜：哇，這裡看得到香港的夜景！

【少年跟著走上高處】

靜：嘿——！香——港——！我——愛——你——！

少年：你講國語佢聽唔明㗎！

靜：那你教我廣東話。

少年：廣東話佢唔 like 㗎。

靜：那她喜歡什麼？

少年：港式英文。

靜：HONG KONG I LOVE U！—

少年：差個 Ar 字，冇 Ar 就唔香港㗎喇。跟我嗌：HONG KONG I 甩 U Ar！

靜：HONG KONG I LOVE U Ar！—

少年：個 love 字唔使咁清楚，HONG KONG I 甩 U Ar！

靜：HONG KONG I LOVE U Ar！

少年：啱喇！

靜：HONG KONG I LOVE U Ar！

　　　HONG KONG I LOVE U Ar！

　　　HONG KONG, I LOVE U Ar.

【停頓】

【少年拿出煙花棒】

少年：玩唔玩啊？

靜：咦，煙花棒？

少年：一陣帶你去個安全啲嘅地方放。

靜：呀哈，真巧！我也有！

【汪靜從手袋裡拿出一盒小型禮炮】

少年：椰子？！

靜：開心嗎？

少年：你居然有咁大粒椰子？

靜：現在放好不好？

少年：喂，砰砰聲響㗎喎，你邊處整㗎㗎？

靜：同事從瀏陽帶給我的，我們家特產啊你忘了嗎？

少年：唔得唔得，你嗰件手榴彈㗎嚟唔可以放。

靜：（嚴肅地）咱湖南人過年必須放花炮。

少年：（嚴肅地）No way. 我唔想坐監呀 —

靜：好吧。

【停頓】

靜：你這個人真沒意思。

【停頓】

少年：Sorry.

【停頓】

【汪靜從錢包拿出一張照片】

靜：這是五年前的我。

少年：……

靜：很不一樣了噢？

少年：係咩？

104

靜：呵。

【停頓】

靜：我老了。

【停頓】

靜：至少是沒以前好看了。

【停頓】

靜：你別告訴我你看不出來我三十多了（粵）細路。

少年：……

靜：難道你看不到我眼角都起皺紋了嗎？我可是已經當媽媽的
　　人啦。

少年：……

靜：胸部都開始下垂了呢。

少年：……

靜：大概老娘還有那麼一點點姿色？

少年：……

【汪靜從後方抱著少年】

靜：女人就跟煙花一樣。

【停頓】

靜：「嘭！」地，就那麼一下下。

【停頓】

靜：沒了。

【停頓】

靜：陪我照兩張相怎樣？

少年：……

靜：天亮我可就走了噢靚仔。

少年：走去邊？

靜：加拿大。

少年：噢，佢要去加拿大？

靜：嗯，他們都説香港很快就不行了。

少年：你要同個二世祖咁繼續落去？

靜：……

少年：我以前講嘅嘢都係嘥氣。

【停頓】

少年：我話過你要 ——

靜：獨立 ——

少年：係。

【停頓】

少年：你可以㗎，俾啲勇氣 ——

靜：我做不到。

少年：係你唔想，你過慣咗呢種／生活喇。

靜：是的，我沒辦法。你要我找份正當的工作每個月領幾千塊
錢還帶著個六歲大的女兒？——

少年：你同佢有結果㗎，佢咁後生，只不過係貪新鮮，遲早㧒
低你！——

靜：所以呢？

少年：離開佢。

【停頓】

靜：呵，你這話，一年前怎麼不説呀？

少年：……

靜：一年前我説要跟他你為什麼／不吭聲？

106

少年：我咩都幫唔到你嘛 ─

靜：我要你什麼了嗎？

少年：……

靜：現在我已經沒辦法了，你卻叫我離開他？

少年：……

靜：為什麼你們男的總在我沒辦法的時候才説話？ ─

少年：個女係你自己要生㗎，係你自己話要攞個女嚟綁實佢老
　　　豆㗎 ─

靜：沒人告訴我綁不住他啊，我現在女兒都沒了。

【停頓】

少年：小柔去咗邊？

靜：我前夫把她從湖南接回台灣了。

少年：……

靜：呼，我現在總算自由了，愛去哪兒去哪兒。

少年：我幫你去搵佢。

靜：呵呵，你要幫我？

少年：我 OK 呀。

靜：呵呵。

少年：唔信我呀？

靜：你真要幫我啊？

少年：……

靜：那你遠遠地看著就好了。

【停頓】

靜：就像看煙花一樣。

【汪靜掏出相機遞給少年】

靜：去拍張照。

少年：……

靜：用閃光燈，走遠點，到最下面去。

少年：……

靜：去啊。

少年：黑麻麻一陣我唔知你企邊呀。

【汪靜點了一支煙】

靜：看到了麼？一會向著這點光就對了。

少年：噢。

靜：等等。

【汪靜將煙塞到少年嘴裡，自己又點了一支】

少年：你知我唔食㗎啦。

靜：含著，我總得知道你走多遠啊。

【少年拿起相機走出兩步】

靜：遠點！再遠點！要照到階梯！還有樹！好了，對對對就那
個位置！

【汪靜揮動手中的煙】

靜：喂！看到我嗎？

少年：OK呀！

【汪靜用煙頭點燃煙花，少年遠遠看見】

少年：喂，呢度唔俾放㗎！

靜：快照！

【停頓】

靜：要燒完了噢，我點另一根了。

少年：得得得！

【少年為汪靜拍照，燈光閃了好幾下】

【煙花燃盡】

【陷入一片黑暗】

少年：喂！熄咗喇！

【停頓】

靜：還有呀！

【汪靜點燃椰子】

【一顆流星劃破夜空，綻放出一朵花】

【火花照亮了一切，少年消失，轉而變成了李可】

【一片黑暗】

【第二顆流星，火花再次照亮，李可轉而變成了男子】

【時空像是沉入了海底，一切都放緩了十倍】

靜：喂——！

男：喂——！

靜：天空開花喇——！

可：聽日坐監喇——！

靜：許個願吧——！

少年：吓——？

靜：流星呀——！

男：咩話——？！

靜：滿天的流星——！

可：你走去邊呀——！

靜：去看清楚一點——！

【汪靜仰望夜空，逐漸上升，似乎就要離開地面】

少年：我嚟幫你啦——！

靜：不要過來——！

可：留低唔得咩——？！

靜：你不需要過來——！

男：我知呀——！

靜：過來你就真沒辦法啦——！

少年：我有呀——！

靜：你有辦法嗎——？！

可：我冇呀——！

靜：那就好好對待我的花吧——！

男：咩花呀——？！

【汪靜丟出一卷長長的白色絲綢，遠遠飛向少年】

靜：這是我繡的流星花——！像嗎——？！

【白色絲綢緩緩展開，薄如蟬翼，沒有任何花紋，它緩緩上升，填滿了整片夜空】

靜：每天繡十朵，三千多朵流星花——！

少年：……

靜：送給你啦——！

可：……

靜：香港的夜好長呀——！

男：……

靜：我天天想，夜夜想，什麼時候能看到流星花——！

少年：……

靜：原來真的有——！

【汪靜雙腳離開了地面】

少年：你唔好郁呀——！

靜：流星會開花——！

可：花咋嘛——！

靜：開花……

少年：好出奇咩——！

靜：就會結果——！

可：唔好睇呀——！

靜：我想看結果——！

少年：結果唔重要㗎——！

靜：我要看結果——！

可：睇唔到點算呀——？！

靜：想看清楚一點——！

少年：唔好再去喇——！

靜：那麼美的花……

可：救你唔㗎喇——！

靜：會結出怎樣的果呢——？！

【男子快步跑向階梯的最高處，緊抱著汪靜的雙腳】

男：冇呀！冇結果㗎！你明唔明呀冇結果㗎冇結果㗎你明唔撚明呀！唔好去嘞，唔好再去嘞，我真係唔得嘞，我冇辦法，再唔講你知會死，真係會死，呢一年我癲咗咁搵女人，日頭搵，半夜搵，有少少時間就去搵，但每一個我都唔滿意，每一個我都唔滿意！我同佢哋做……唔係，係搞，然後俾錢。「唔係，呢樣唔係我要嘅嘢唔係我要嘅」，每一次搞完我都有呢種 feel，我有試過呃自己，但呢把聲死都唔肯消失！「唔係我要嘅唔係我要嘅」，每一次都加重我傷口嘅發作，但就係唔敢承認自己嘅無膽無能同無恥，我完全唔明點解會變成宜家個撚樣，我從嚟冇覺得自己好似宜家咁犯賤咁虛偽咁假。我真係想死，死撚咗就好嘞！我

111

心入邊一直諗，咁嘅地獄仲要去到幾時！直至喘先你攬著我，就好似我宜家攬著你咁。

【第十五場完】

第十六場　一支煙

第十六場　一支煙

【無燈】

【一根火柴被劃燃】

【出現了一支煙，深吸了一口，在黑暗中隱隱發光】

（粵）他點了一支煙，半空中騰起一襲迂迴縈繞的白色絲綢，他的眼神在氤氳中飄忽不定，於是，這輕紗曼舞捲著他的腰，牽著他飄出窗外，飄向那沉睡的天際。他輕輕推開蓬鬆的雲層，游向那時現時隱的星火，卻發現，天空的那一面，是無數像他一樣的人，每個人都站在自己的星球上，在發呆，在沉思，在不安……不約而同的是，他們手上都夾著一支煙。有的深吸一口，於是夜空偶爾會傳來短暫而明亮的螢火；有的一口一口，淡淡地抽，於是遠處便總有那微弱而延續的星光。星星點點，遠遠近近，是一顆顆相距不知多少光年的星球，是一個個永遠觸不到對方的守望者，是一支支抽不完燃不盡的香煙。

（粵）他不寂寞了，遙望著這星光點點。可他孤獨了，他別無辦法，唯有也點燃一支煙，向遠方的遠方發出微弱的信號。或許，大家都同時深吸一口，同時深深地寂寞，天空會被照亮，黑暗會被驅逐。可惜，大家都看不到彼此的信號，更無法契合，唯有將這一整夜的寂寥汲入胸腔，在黎明到來之前，吐出一朵可以乘涼的雲。

【第十六場完】

第十七場　蛻變

第十七場　蛻變

時間：回到第一場，凌晨五點。
地點：男子的居所。
人物：少年、少女。

【窗外的雨已經停了，偶爾有一兩點雨滴「嗒、嗒」地打在窗上】
【少女獨自一人，坐在床上化妝，茶几上擺放了一張千元港幣】
【少年從浴室出來，擦著頭髮】
【少年拿起吹風筒吹頭髮】
【少女收拾著自己的物品】
【少年打開音響，隱隱傳來 Coldplay 的〝Yellow〞】
【少年倒了杯水，坐到床邊，遞給少女】
女：唔使喇。
【停頓】
女：尋晚真係好大雨呀。
少年：係呀。
【停頓】
少年：唔好意思。
女：吓？
少年：過晒鐘添……
女：呵，預咗喇。
【停頓】
女：你話香港會唔會水浸呢？
少年：……

116

女：如果水浸，我諗全香港人都會好攰開心。

少年：……

女：地鐵停晒啦，巴士停晒啦，關口封晒啦，街面姓周嗰啲檔口執晒啦，唔會再有啲強國人係咁湧晒入嚟搶金啦，所有香港市民都可以騎隻大黃鴨出嚟扒下艇仔遊下船河啦……

【少女收拾完畢】

女：好啦。

【少女拿起茶几上的一千港幣，塞進錢包】

女：我要走了。

少年：哦……

【停頓】

少年：係喇……

【少年將手錶遞給少女】

【停頓】

【少女接過】

【停頓】

【少女拿出魔方】

女：砌好咗喇……

【少年去接，少女不給】

女：有冇人話過你長氣㗎？

少年：吓？

女：你……好攰多嘢講。

少年：哦。

【停頓】

少年：可能太耐冇講嘢喇呱。

女：太耐？

少年：係呀……幾耐喇…都。

【停頓】

【少女將魔方遞給少年】

女：其實我記得㗎。

少年：咩？

女：嚟之前同你傾過好多嘢……

少年：呵……

女：不過……未見過……有啲緊張……

【停頓】

女：講個秘密你知呀。

少年：吓？

【少女靠近少年，輕輕耳語】

【少年注視著少女】

【停頓】

少年：嘩。

女：（國）是真的。

【停頓】

女：（國）你一定要信我。

【停頓】

少年：呵。

女：呵呵。

【傳來稀稀落落的鳥鳴】

女：雀仔都叫喇，呵呵。

【少女開一扇窗，窗外一片汪洋】

【少女深呼吸】

【停頓】

女：早晨呀香港。

少年：早晨……

女：早晨呀香港！！！

【傳來各種不同的回音】

【遠處，有的人在划船，有的人在游泳】

女：你估呢度游去天水圍幾耐呢？

少年：兩個……三個鐘？

女：哈，游到都未必上到岸吖。

【停頓】

少年：有冇散紙？

女：吓？

【少年拿出幾個硬幣放在少女手中】

少年：去搭天星小輪。

女：吓？

少年：不過你要游去碼頭先㗎……

女：……

少年：使唔使我送？

【停頓】

女：（國）你遠遠地看著就好喇。

【兩人看著窗外】

【男子拿起模型建築走到窗邊，探出窗外將其放在水面】

【模型載著河馬公仔靜靜漂向遠處】

【一輪紅日從海面緩緩升起】

女：隻歌唱緊咩呀？

少年：……吓？

【停頓】

【歌一邊唱，少年不太自信地一邊解釋。】

少年：望住粒星啦……

【停頓】

少年：望住佢哋為你係咁閃係咁閃啦……

【停頓】

少年：無論你做咩都係咁閃係咁閃啦……

【停頓】

少年：耶……佢哋全部都好驚青……

【停頓】

少年：我一路跟住你㗎……

【停頓】

少年：寫隻歌仔俾你㗎……

【停頓】

少年：是但你做咩我都寫㗎……

【停頓】

少年：個歌名就叫……《驚青》……

【停頓】

少年：然後我會落定決心……

【停頓】

少年：想搞掂你㗎……

【停頓】

少年：但我又開始……

【停頓】

少年：驚青喎……

【少年繼續著】

【一道紅潤的晨光透過玻璃窗照進屋子，燒紅了一整片】

【牆上，投射了一道黑影，在一片紅光中緩慢爬行】

【是壁虎的影子】

【劇終】

Characters

Man, unemployed and on social security assistance, in his 30s
Girl, the **Man's** internet friend
Li Ke, an insurance salesman and private tutor, in his 20s
Qin Yun, a woman from Fujian adrift in Hong Kong, in her 20s
Boy, a secondary school graduate
Wang Jing, a woman from Hunan adrift in Hong Kong, in her 30s

The / denotes the overlapping point where the next line begins.

The – at the end of a line marks the point of interruption by another character.

The ... signals a trailing off when a character is hesitating, thinking or hinting at something.

Qin Yun speaks Cantonese with a slight accent. She speaks in Cantonese unless otherwise stated.

Wang Jing speaks in Mandarin unless otherwise stated.

Other characters speak in Cantonese unless otherwise stated.

Scene 1 **Rendezvous**

Scene 1   Rendezvous

Time: late at night in spring

*Place: the **Man**'s flat*

*Characters: **Man**, **Girl***

A standard studio.

*The **Man** is arranging something.*

Standing on a stool, he opens the wall cupboard. He grabs a bottle of red wine and a bottle of vodka. He thinks.

He puts the red wine back, then puts the vodka into the fridge. He checks his watch.

He takes out a bottle of cologne and puts some on.

He sits down on the sofa and puts on some music.

Drawing the speakers close, he loses himself in the music.

There is a quiet knocking. He doesn't seem to notice.

Suddenly, he snaps out of his reverie and opens the door.

*The **Girl**, with the air of a slightly bookish student, stands in the doorway.*

Girl   Hi.

Pause.

Man   Hi…

Pause.

He realises he should let her in. He moves aside.

She comes in and starts to take her shoes off.

Man   Nah, it's all right.

He closes the door.

Girl   Did you put that on especially? –

She leans in and sniffs.

Girl   Boss?

Man   …

Girl   Dunhill?

Man   …

Girl   Dior? Davidoff? Versace? –

Man   I… just put whatever on.

Girl   …

Man   Do sit. Drink?

*The **Girl** notices the gecko on the window just when she's about to sit down.*

Girl   What is that?!

Man   Oh, it's all right…

Girl   That's a really fat lizard!

Man   Gecko.

Girl   What?

Man   Gecko. Common house gecko.

Girl   Can you get rid of it?

Man   It's dead. It's not gonna move.

He digs around in the fridge.

Man What do you fancy?

*The **Girl** sits on the stool opposite the sofa.*

Man Lemon tea? Soda water?

Girl …

Man Coffee? Tea? Coke? Lemonade?

Girl Whatever.

Man Got cake too. Want some?

Girl Wh… what do you think about me?

Man Eh?

Girl My looks.

Pause.

Man Cor, you're forward –

Girl It's not the first day you've known me.

Man Sort of. This is the first time we've met.

She checks her watch.

He takes some moon cakes and the vodka from the fridge and puts them on the coffee table.

Girl Why did it die there?

Man Burnt by the sun.

Girl Burnt?

Man It got stuck on the window –

Girl Eek…

Man Look, its tail was torn –

Girl Can you make it go away?

Pause.

Girl   Please.

He closes the curtains.

Man   Sorted.

Girl   What're you playing?

Man   Coldplay –

Girl   It all sounds the same –

Man   I like to loop this –

Girl   Can you turn it down? –

Man   Sorry.

He puts it on mute.

Girl   Thank you. What's that?

Man   … cake.

Girl   … moon cake?

Man   … it's all cake.

Girl   It's only March…

Man   Sorry, that's all I've got. It's edible… just –

Pause.

She takes her phone from her bag and checks her watch.

He glances at her.

Man   You don't look like that.

Girl *(laughs)*   Huh?

Man   The pictures you sent on WeChat… look like Angelababy…

Girl   And?

Man   You… look like a schoolgirl…

Pause.

Girl   Stand up.

Pause.

Girl   Stand.

He stands. She embraces him.

After a moment, she lets go.

Girl (*gently*)   Relax. Don't be so nervous.

She sits down.

Girl   Why're you still standing? Sit.

He sits.

Girl   Better?

Man   Eh?

Girl   You're either lonely or just been dumped.

Man   How old are you?

Girl   Guess.

Man   Oh.

Girl   Ha, interesting.

Man   Me?

Girl   Got moon cakes and vodka out for me.

Man   Oh sorry, I forgot the glasses.

He digs out a big bowl and pushes it over to her.

Man   Sorry, can't find a glass.

Girl   Give me a glass of water, please.

He pours her a bowl of water.

Girl   Do I really look that young?

Man It's just looks. Won't be surprised if you've got a baby, ha ha.

Girl How do you know?

Man … eh?

Girl What else did I tell you?

Pause.

Man You said –

Girl He's such a hassle –

Man …

Girl You'll have to feed him, help him poo –

Man I see.

Girl Make sure he doesn't bite –

Man I… eh?

Pause.

Girl Baby is my dog.

Man I see.

Pause.

Man How did you train it? It knows what to do when it needs to wee?

Pause.

Girl Is this how you chat up girls?

Man …

Girl It's weird talking to you –

Man Sorry –

Girl Don't need to –

Man Sorry –

Girl   OK, stop. Can... can you remember... Isn't there something you want to tell me?

Man   Mm?

Girl   You know... not about pets.

Man   Yeah...

Girl   Can you remember...

She checks her phone.

Girl   ... the things we said on WeChat?

Man   'Course, loads. We chatted lots before this.

Girl   Yeah, yeah.

Man   Hobbies, dreams, annoyances...

Girl   Yeah, yeah.

Pause.

Man   Phew! I thought you've turned into another person. Meeting for the first time / is a bit awkward...

Girl   Wait.

Man   What?

Girl   Annoyances.

Man   Eh?

Girl   Go on. Can you remember what I said?

Man   ... yeah.

Girl   What then?

Man   ... you need money?

Girl   No.

Man   No?

Girl   I need to help someone sick back home.

Man   So…?

Girl   You said… you want to help.

Man   … yeah. Yeah?

Girl   Yeah.

Man   Oh.

Girl   So… now…

Man   Eh?

She smiles.

Girl   Don't worry…

Man   What?

Girl   I know what to do.

Man   Do… what?

Girl   You.

Silence.

Man   … sorry.

Girl   …

Man   Is there a… misunderstanding?

Girl   Huh?

Man   All the time we've talked, I don't recall…

Girl   …

Man   I thought… we've…

Girl   What?

Man   Got something in common.

Girl   … yeah.

Man   Or we got along well, yeah?

Girl   … yeah.

Man   Do you remember… I… we said, come up if you're free…

Girl   Yeah.

Man   For a drink…

Girl   Yeah.

Man   Talk…

Girl   Yeah.

Pause.

Girl   And?

Man   And… and what?

Girl   There's no 'and'? Then why did you ask me here this late at night?

Man   To talk.

Girl   Talk? I'm this pretty and you asked me here to talk?

Man   Is that illegal?

Girl   And?

Man   …

Girl   There's no 'and'?

Man   …

Girl   You want me to believe you… that there's no 'and'?

He takes his phone out.

Man   No, no. Well, maybe we can check our WeChat record –

Girl   I charge.

Pause.

Girl   I'm not here for a laugh.

Pause.

Girl   Clear?

Silence.

Man   So… is this… compensated dating?

Pause.

Girl   Call it anything you want.

Man   I really didn't –

Girl   Yeah right.

Pause.

Girl   Everyone's doing it. And you tell me you don't know?

Silence.

Man   Sorry.

Girl   …

Man   Looks like it really is a misunderstanding.

Girl   …

Man   Sorry to have wasted your time.

Girl   …

Man   You… you should go now.

Girl   Are you taking the piss?

Silence.

She takes her bag and heads for the door.

He looks hesitant. He takes a deep breath.

Man   No, come back…

Girl   …

Man   Sorry, I thought…

She looks at him.

Man   Come back… sit down, please.

She moves slowly back to the sofa and sits down.

Man   Sorry.

She takes her phone out.

Girl   This is what I charge.

She types it into the phone.

Girl   I've got things to do in two hours.

Man   That's really late.

Girl   So?

Man   What've you got to do?

She moves next to him and puts her hand on his thigh.

Girl   You'll find out soon…

She then lifts her hand and signals for money.

Man   All the things we've talked about…

Girl   Uh-huh?

Man   You… don't feel anything?

Girl   What do you want me to feel?

Man   I…

Girl   Uh-huh?

Man   I saw you as a friend…

Girl   Am I… not?

Man   Why don't we talk a bit more, get to know each other?

Pause.

Girl   Cunt! Should've said earlier if you've got no money!

She gets up to leave.

He stands up and gets a $1,000 note from his wallet.

Man   Here's a thousand. The other one, in a bit.

Pause.

Man   Sit.

She sits.

Girl   You really are special.

Pause.

Man   Right, what were you saying just now?

Girl   You really / are…

Man   No, no, before that.

Girl   Should've said earlier / if you've…

Man   No no no, there's another word.

Girl *(inhales)* …

Man   From now on, I don't want to hear that word again, OK?

Silence.

He pours her a bowl of vodka.

Man   Drink.

Pause.

She sips a tiny bit.

Silence.

She stands up and looks around.

Girl Looks all right here. Quite tidy.

Man Thanks.

Girl How long have you been here?

Man Eh… a while –

Girl Renting?

Man 'Course.

Girl Horrible outside though. Stinks.

Man Oh, babies piss out there.

Girl Huh?

Man I'm talking about dogs.

Girl Oh…

Man If I see it, I'll pick it up for hot pot.

Pause.

Girl If you hate dogs so much, why do you still live here?

Man It's cheap.

Girl Oh yeah, perfect for you out here.

Pause.

Girl You work?

Man … don't have a job.

Silence.

She sees an unfinished model on top of the fridge. It's a house. A toy hippo sits inside. A Rubik's Cube sits next to the house.

Girl That hippo looks bloody daft.

Man …

Girl Just like you.

Man   How?

Girl   That squint.

Man   Ha.

Girl   You like to make these?

She moves over to take a good look.

Man   Yeah, everything…

Girl   Oh, it's not finished.

Man   Cards, Rubik's Cubes…

Girl   Wow, it's paper. That's fun.

Man   This one took me a whole month. A whole damn month.

He passes the Rubik's Cube to her.

Pause.

She takes it.

Girl   You don't have a job?

Man   Yeah.

She crumbles the Rubik's Cube and puts it back into his hand as if nothing has happened.

Girl   Now you've got something to do.

She takes the model down.

Man *(sternly)*   Don't – you – dare.

Girl   Who's this for?

Man   …

Girl   A pretty girl?

Man   …

Girl A northern chick?

Man …

Girl A little girl?

Man …

Girl Your first love?

Man …

Girl Say something.

Man …

Girl I'm trying here.

Man …

Girl Unhappy?

Man …

Girl Why?

Man …

Girl Tell me what's upsetting you.

Man Why don't I ask you something…

Girl Shoot.

Man Why do you choose to do this?

Pause.

Girl Baby's sick.

End of Scene 1.

Scene 2 A Wondrous Place

Scene 2   A Wondrous Place

The **Boy** *alone.*

Boy   I never realised I'd become what I am today. What I really want to know is how we change, slowly and gradually – or maybe I should say, evolve? From homo erectus to homo sapiens. After such a bloody long evolution, I want to know: as a tiny part in this long process, what have I achieved? Just like when you ask a hairdresser to shave off all your hair. At which point do you become a bona fide baldy? I've actually been thinking about this bloody daft question all the time. Perhaps it's because, I, this, have silently started to change.

The narrator becomes the **Man**.

Man   That day, I walk past an alleyway. One so deep that you can't see the end. I'm always intrigued by things so deep that you can't see the end. So I scamper down and walk up a starry, dazzling stairway. Wafts of fragrance rush at me, familiar and mysterious.

After an hour, I sit on the edge of her bed. My left hand stroking her long hair and my right holding her hand, 'It's time for me to go,' I say. I kiss her, leave my number, and a few hundreds.

End of Scene 2.

Scene 3 **Take Flight**

Scene 3   Take Flight

Time: a summer afternoon several years ago
Place: **Li Ke**'s *flat*
Characters: **Li Ke**, **Qin Yun**

Li Ke's *flat. The door is flung open.* **Qin Yun** *enters, kicks her heels to one side and collapses onto the sofa.* **Li Ke** *staggers in with his phone between his head and shoulder, dragging a suitcase. He shuts the door as he talks.*

Ke *(rapidly)*   Hey, Mrs Chan, to be frank, I only do tutoring, I don't deal with other problems. Well, I can talk a little, we'll deduct the time from your daughter's lesson. Putting it plainly, her grades are bad because she doesn't want to study but you force her and the more you force her the less she wants to study so in other words she's off her rockers because of this. (Pause.) Actually, I'm also in insurance, if you're worried that the new system will affect her academic future, I highly recommend this end-of-an-era certificate protection product… can't understand? Mandarin? All right…

He takes a deep breath.

Ke *(in Mandarin)*   Linda's off her rockers from studying. *(Pause.)* She needs insurance.

Pause.

Ke *(in Mandarin)*   Linda's your daughter. That's her English name. Mrs Chan, sorry, my boss's calling. Talk later.

He turns off the phone, exhales deeply.

Ke   Sorry.

He puts away the suitcase and looks at her.

Ke   What do you want to drink?

Pause.

Ke   Water?

Pause.

Ke   Something fizzy?

Pause.

Ke   Lemonade?

Pause.

Ke   You can stay here tonight.

Yun   …

Ke   Have you got a towel? Shall I grab one?

Yun   …

He sits on the sofa's arm, caressing her hair.

Ke   Shower?

Yun   I'm shagged… shagged…

Silence.

Yun   Last Chinese train's at eight, right?

Ke   Yeah.

She checks her watch.

Yun   It's a mess. My head's going to pop.

Silence.

Yun   My dear sis lured me here. Dear ol' sis, you stinking cunt, you bugger off to make big bucks and I get locked up in a tiny room for four whole days, staring at four bleeding walls. It's dark and dingy and I can't go anywhere. It's like being in jail. That cock of a boss wanted money for rent and food. Fuck you, I work four whole fucking days and I make just enough to get back. *(In Mandarin)* You fuckhead, think missy is a ditsy cunt, huh?

Ke   You want go back?

Yun   I wanna go now. This missy dragged that shit down 14 floors in the fire escape just to jump ship. *(In Mandarin)* These motherfucking Hong Kong streets all look the fucking same. Drive me round the bend, going 'round scaring folks with all this paint on me face.

Pause.

Yun   You're the only number I've got –

Ke   At your service.

Yun   If you're messing with me you're dead meat.

Pause.

Yun   You teach?

Ke   Yep, part-time. Haven't met one?

Yun   I know lots.

Pause.

Ke   You want a shower?

Yun   I'm starving.

Ke   Leave your things here, we'll grab something.

Yun   What? Curry beef?

Ke   Ha.

Yun   Can't see what so great about this hole. Food's awful.
           But everyone's dying to move here.

Ke   C'mon, I'll take you to somewhere good.

Pause.

Ke   Have you been to the Harbour? We can go later, it's
           really pretty –

Yun   No.

Ke   It's a wasted trip if you haven't been.

Yun   I've got a train to catch.

Ke   Plenty of time.

Yun   If you're messing with me you're dead meat.

Pause.

Yun   What harbour –

Ke   Victoria Harbour –

Yun   What's there to see?

Ke   The sea, a park, the Avenue of Stars – got loads of film
           star hand prints there.

Yun   Who?

Ke   Loads.

Yun   Stephen Chow?

Ke   For sure.

Yun   Ooh I like him. Andy Lau?

Ke   For sure.

Yun   I like him. Tsang Chi-wai?

Ke   For sure.

Yun   Is he that fucking tiny?

Ke   Yeah.

Yun   Is Andy Lau that fucking cool?

Ke   Oh yeah.

She yawns and stretches, her arm reaches toward the window behind her.

Yun *(slightly coyly)*   Who else…

She looks around and notices the gecko on the window. She jumps.

Yun   Blimey!

Ke   You jumped really high.

Yun   What's that?!

Ke   Gecko.

Yun   Why's it burnt?!

Ke   The sun.

Yun   Blimey! Enough.

She puts on her shoes.

Ke   Where are you going?

Yun   To see Stephen Chow!

End of Scene 3.

Scene 4 Bamboo Horse

Scene 4   Bamboo Horse

Time: early evening of the same day

Place: a children's playground near the Victoria Harbour

Characters: same as previous scene

Ke   Look at yourself.

Yun   That's awful. Delete.

Ke   Ha ha, you bumpkin.

Yun   Delete.

Ke   So damn bumpkin.

Yun   Delete.

Ke   Look at this. Your hands are so fucking enormous.

Yun   That's really Tsang Chi-wai's hand?

Ke   Yeah.

Yun   They're so fucking cute. His hands!

Ke   He's tiny.

Yun   So cute! I never thought he's that short. I mean, that
           short. That fucking short. Why did his mum make him
           so fucking damn short? Ha ha ha!

Ke   Fancy a drink?

*He touches his Octopus card on the vending machine. It's not
responding.*

Ke   Hm, not working.

He smacks the vending machine.

Yun   Hey, have you seen any Stephen Chow films? The one about him coming to Hong Kong for the first time to buy water.

Ke   No, show me.

Yun   'Sir, sir, first time here. Do be kind and give us a few mouthfuls of water.'

Silence.

Two bottles of lemon tea come out of the machine.

Yun   Hey.

Pause.

Yun   I'm going to play in that park!

Ke *(gestures at the bottle)*   Do you know this?

Yun   No.

Ke   You must've seen the ad when you were young, 'Eh? What a coincidence?'

Yun   Erm, no.

Ke   How did you find out about Stephen Chow then?

Yun   Tudou.

Pause.

Yun   Wah, I wanna go on the swing! Fuck me, how come that kid's so damn fast?

Ke   Come here. This is really fun.

He sits on the spring horse.

Ke   Yeehaw!

Yun   …

Ke   Yeehaw! Come! Get on this! It's great.

Yun   Cor, you're fucking nuts.

Ke   Come!

Yun   You really are fucking nuts!

Ke   C'mon! Chase me!

Yun   Ha ha ha ha!

She mounts a spring horse.

Yun   Yeehaw!

They chase each other in high spirits.

Suddenly, everything seems to slow down 10 times. They seem to be racing inside a giant lump of jelly.

Ke   Hey – !

Yun   Yeehaw – !

Ke   Hey – !

Yun   Yeehaw – !

Ke   Missy – !

Yun   Huh – ?

Ke   Where are you from – ?

Yun   You don't need to know – ! Yeehaw – !

Ke   Yeehaw – ! Why – ?

Yun   'Cause I don't know myself – !

Ke   I'll help – !

Yun   You can't – ! Yeehaw – !

Ke   Yeehaw – ! Stop – !

Yun   Can't – !

Ke   Where are you going – ?

Yun   Back – !

Ke   Where – ?

Yun   Don't know – ! Yeehaw – !

Ke   Yeehaw – ! The sun's setting. Stop for a bit – !

Yun   Can't – !

Ke   My horse is shagged – !

Yun   Can't help you – !

She leaps down and into a river.

This river seems to be also made out of jelly.

Ke   Hey – !

He follows.

Ke   Where are you going – ?

Yun   Back – !

Ke   It's all wrong – !

Yun   Whatever – !

Ke   The Island's over there – !

Yun   Raze it flat – !

Ke   Stop – !

Yun   So free – !

Ke   It'll be the Pacific – !

Yun   So peaceful – !

Ke   It's completely dark now – !

Yun   That's even better, we can see clearer – !

Ke   We can't get back – !

Yun   We will – ! The world's round – !

She climbs onto a new continent, running like the wind.

This continent seems to be made out of jelly too.

He follows.

They pant. Returns to normal speed.

Ke   Oi! Aren't you tired?

Yun   Hang on!

Ke   Onto what?

Yun   Don't give up!

Ke   Give what up?

Yun   Almost there!

Ke   Where?

Yun   Nearly over!

Ke   What's over?

Yun   Can't you see?

Ke   What?

Yun   Shooting stars!

Ke   Where?

Yun   Grab onto its tail!

Ke   Where?

Yun   That shooting star's losing its tail!

Ke   It's a plane!

Yun   Run after it!

Ke   Run?

Yun   It can fly!

Ke   It's not going to stop!

Yun   Will it keep flying?!

Ke   The sun's almost out!

Yun   No!

Ke   It's almost bright!

Yun   I don't want it!

Ke   Now!

Yun   Run! If you don't run now, you'll never catch up!

He stops.

End of Scene 4.

Scene 5 Idiot

Scene 5 Idiot

Time: eight o'clock in the evening of the same day

Place: **Li Ke**'s *flat*

Characters: same as previous scene

Following immediately from the previous scene.

The metal gate is pulled open. **Qin Yun** *rushes over to her suitcase.*

Yun   It's your fault if I don't catch it, you fucker.

Li Ke *closes the door and leans against it.*

Ke   You won't make it –

Yun   Don't fucking care –

Ke   Definitely won't make it –

Yun   I have to leave here – now.

She drags her suitcase to the door. He grabs her hand.

Ke   Stay with me tonight?

Yun   I want to go home.

Silence.

He lets go.

Ke   Go, go, I don't like to force…

Silence.

She lets go of her suitcase, thinking about giving him a hug.

He pulls her into an embrace and kisses her.

Yun   What you playing at?

Ke   What now?

Pause.

Yun   What you playing at?

Ke   What now?

Yun   If you're messing with me you're dead meat –

Ke   Then why did you come? –

Yun   For my things.

Ke   And?

Yun   Go.

Ke   And now?

She struggles. He's not letting go.

Yun   Let go.

She struggles. He's not letting go.

Yun   Let go of me. Call yourself a teacher?

She struggles. He's not letting go.

Yun   You men are all scumbags! –

Ke   Bang on.

Yun (*in Mandarin*)   You're all fucking bastards! –

Ke   Yeah.

Yun (*in Mandarin*)   Fuck you bastards! –

Ke   Yeah.

Yun (*in Mandarin*)   Wimpy bastards! –

Ke   What?

He lets go. They stare at each other.

Yun   What d'ya want?

He kisses her.

She pushes him away.

Yun   What if someone fancies you?

Pause.

Ke   If you dare, I've got the balls too.

Pause.

Yun *(in Mandarin)*   Liar.

Ke   What now?

Yun   You think I'm retarded.

He kisses her.

She pushes him away and points at him.

Yun   You'll regret this for life.

He kisses her.

She pushes him away and points at him again.

Yun   I'm telling you now, I'm not like the others. I'll stick to you, tight. *(In Mandarin)* Even if you run to the end of the world, turn into dust, I'll dig you up!

Pause.

Yun   Scared?

Ke   Ha.

Yun   I'm telling you, if you're m…

He drags her onto the bed.

They struggle.

He tries to take her clothes off.

She slaps him.

Pause.

He smiles.

She slaps him again.

He burrows down. She gradually stops fighting.

He takes her clothes off.

She turns off the lights.

He turns them back on.

She turns them off again.

Ke   What're you doing?

Yun   Let it be.

Ke   Shy?

Yun   I like this.

He resumes.

End of Scene 5.

Scene 6 My Name

Scene 6   My Name

Time: late at night of the same day

Place: **Li Ke**'s *flat*

Characters: same as previous scene

A messy bedroom.

Li Ke *lies diagonally across the bed. His eyes shut, breathing heavily.*

Qin Yun *is standing next to the coffee table in his t-shirt. She looks as energetic as ever.*

She pours a glass of water and gulps it down.

She looks around the room.

She pours another glass of water and gives it to him.

Yun   Why don't you put on cologne?

Ke   Eh?

Yun   How come an educated man like you don't wear cologne?

Ke   What?

Yun   Don't see me without cologne next time.

Ke   Eh?

Yun   Got any fags?

He takes out his cigarettes and lighter, and lights one for her.

Ke   I thought you didn't smoke.

Yun   How come you didn't smoke today?

Ke   'Cause… it tastes funny when you snog –

Yun   You had that planned?

Ke   Is that a problem?

Yun   Hrrmph.

Silence.

She takes a toy hippo out of her bag.

Yun   Looks similar, no?

Ke   Who?

Yun   You.

Ke   Me? How? I don't have a belly.

Yun   That bloody daftness. You're just as bloody daft.

Ke   Eh?

Yun   And.

Ke   What?

Yun   Lechy.

Ke   Can't tell.

Yun   His eyes are small like yours.

Ke   Huh?

Yun   For you.

Pause.

Yun   If you lose it, I'll cut your cock off.

He picks it up to take a good look.

Yun   Hey, I think you should put him there…

She takes the hippo and puts it inside the model house on top of the fridge.

Yun   There.

Pause.

Yun   Perfect. Now he's got somewhere to live.

She sits down next to him.

He takes the cigarette from her.

Ke   Don't smoke the last third.

Pause.

Ke   Tell me about you.

Yun   Me?

Ke   Things about you?

Yun   Why?

Ke   Want to get to know you.

Yun   Why do you suddenly want to do that?

Ke   I want to. I don't even know your name.

Yun   Didn't I tell you already? –

Ke   Ferrari? Don't kid me.

Yun   What's the problem?

Ke   No one's really called Ferrari.

Yun   What's Ferrari?

Pause.

Ke   Car.

Yun   Pricey?

Ke   Very. Very few can afford one.

Yun   Wow, aren't you fucking lucky?

Ke   Ha.

He looks at her.

Ke   You're stunning.

Yun   I know.

Ke   Ha.

Yun   It's obvious. You don't have to say it.

Ke   Ha.

Pause.

Yun   My name is Yun.

Ke   Yun? Which one?

Yun   I can write it. Have you got a pen? I'll write it down for you.

He passes her a pen and a Post-it note.

Yun   Think it's like this, Yun, right?

Ke   Yea… I'm not sure.

Yun   What? Aren't you a teacher?

Ke   … this is simplified –

Yun   It's horrible.

Ke   You… don't know how to write?

Yun   … I never went to school.

Pause.

Ke   You're lucky. I'll be your tutor.

Yun   Yeah right.

Ke   See, I'll stick your name with the hippo there.

Yun   What for?

Ke   So I can see you often.

He sticks the Post-it note onto the hippo's forehead.

Pause.

Yun   Ha ha.

Ke   What so funny?

Yun   Like a zombie.

Pause.

Yun   Hippo zombie.

Pause.

Yun   Zombie hippo.

Pause.

Yun   Ha ha.

Pause.

Ke   Why didn't you go to school?

Silence.

Yun   I'm an orphan.

End of Scene 6.

Scene 7 **Red Candle**

Scene 7   Red Candle

Time: same as previous scene

Place: same as previous scene

Characters: **Qin Yun**

Following immediately from the previous scene.

Qin Yun *alone.*

Yun *(in Mandarin)*   I'm an orphan. My foster parents tell me
since I was little that I'd marry their son when I grow
up. One day, brother says he wants a fried egg late at
night, so I light a red candle and go into the kitchen. He
comes in when I'm just heating up the pan. He comes
up close from behind, his pungent alcohol breath shoots
into my ears. 'Come, wife.' As he speaks, he pushes
me onto the floor. I feel numb. I stay still. Buttons come
off. My upper body burns in pain like it's on fire. A red
liquid drips, one drop, two… like arrows, they pierce
into my neck, my breasts, my stomach… Oh, what's
this? I don't know so I close my eyes… You must
think I'm scared. At first, yes. But when your world is
all about doing laundry, cooking, chopping firewood
and feeding pigs, then you'd know how precious that
trembling ecstasy is. We always start out scared, but
once you've overcome yourself, you'd realise that
within the fear, there are many good things that no
one knows about. Brother leaves home to study and
candles just vanish. I need it every night. That flickering

light, dreamlike. That warm liquid dripping onto my chest – congealing, clinging, embracing me. Oh, such joy! This is happiness… I become scared! Scared that I'd be chained here forever. So… I run away. *(In Cantonese)* I've been stuck there for 10 odd years and managed to get away. Beyond the village, there's the town. Beyond the town, there's the city. Beijing, Shanghai, Shenzhen, Hong Kong. I work in factories, massage parlours. I do everything and I'm willing to do anything. Everything. Even things others don't want to do, I've done them all.

End of Scene 7.

Scene 8 Habit

Scene 8   Habit

Time: back to Scene 1

*Place: the **Man**'s flat*

*Characters: **Man**, **Girl***

*The **Man** and the **Girl** are smoking. They are both a bit tipsy.*
He is playing with the Rubik's Cube.

Girl   God, it's so hot.

Man   Bit stuffy.

Girl   It's your vodka.

She takes off her jacket.

Man   Might rain soon.

Girl   Open the window please.

He opens the curtains and the window.

Girl   You're a private tutor.

Man   Was.

Girl   And sell insurance?

Man   Yeah.

Girl   You do everything.

Man   Yeah, Starbucks, PCCW, MTR, water delivery…

Girl   Why are you unemployed?

Man   …

Girl   How do you pay your rent?

Man   …

Girl   Oh, you're on –

Man   The dole.

Girl   …

Man   My whole fucking family are on it.

Girl   Oh, you've signed –

Man   Yeah, declared myself an ingrate.

Girl   …

Man   Eat well, live well, sleep easy. Life's super.

Girl   …

Man   Come, have some. It's free.

She checks her watch.

Man   So, your trade… is it easy to get your feet onto dry land –

Girl   What do you mean?

Man   Compensated dating.

Pause.

Girl   You seem to know it well.

Man   Well, I've seen a bit.

Girl   Don't tell me Qin Yun got herself a sugar daddy.

Man   You think so?

Girl   How would I know?

Man   What do you think then?

Girl   I don't need one.

Pause.

Man   Are you really doing this for your dog?

Girl	Yeah.
Man	…
Girl	Surprising?
Man	…
Girl	For my Baby, I'd do anything.
Man	…
Girl	You won't understand.
Man	I had a dog when I was a kid.
Girl	…
Man	I was playing under the bridge. A box is bobbing up and down in the river, strange sounds are coming from it. I get closer. There's a puppy lying upside down. He sees me and yelps weakly. He looks like he can smile, really bloody cute. So I sneak him home, feed him some Po Chai Pills and hide him under the bed.
Girl	You've got a heart –
Man	He dies the next morning.
Girl	…
Man	I don't know what to do with the body, so I leave it there under the bed. Doesn't take long before it stinks like hell. Flies invade the room. And my dad beats the crap out of me.
Girl	You poor thing… were you devastated?
Man	I really regret it.
Girl	You've done no wrong.

Pause.

Man   Actually I've told you a little before.

Girl   I know.

Man   You know?

Girl   I remember. You said you don't know how to get along with people sometimes.

Man   Yeah.

Girl   That's why I'm here to help you.

Pause.

Man   Did you ever see me as…

Girl   …

Man   You really can't remember…

Girl   Huh?

Man   …

He sets down the Rubik's Cube, picks up a machine to roll a cigarette.

Man   Qin Yun went looking for work near her brother's office.

Girl   Huh? Why did she do that?

She glances at her watch.

Man   That's a nice watch. You like wearing them?

Pause.

Girl   Kind of –

Man   Can I see?

She takes off the watch and gives it to him.

He puts it on and resumes rolling his cigarette.

Girl   Why did she go find her brother?

Man I didn't say that.

Girl Then why did she move near him?

Man To find him.

Pause.

Girl Fine, if you don't want to talk.

She checks her watch, but it's gone.

Girl …

Pause.

Girl If there's nothing else, I'm going.

Man She went to look after him.

Girl Why?

Pause.

Girl What's wrong with her?

Pause.

She lifts her hand, realising her watch is gone, so she flicks her hair instead.

She looks up and sees him looking intently at her.

Man You've taken the money. I do have a request…

He throws her the Rubik's Cube.

Man Fix this, thanks.

Pause.

She starts to play with the Rubik's Cube.

The sound of rain hitting the windows.

It's getting stronger.

He closes the window and looks out – or at the gecko on the window.

Girl   And?

Man   She got stuck.

Girl   Stuck? Why?

Man   He stuck to her.

Girl   What did he do?

Man   Spent all her money.

Girl   She gave him money?

He lights a rollie and takes a drag.

Girl   Why did she do that?

Pause.

Girl   Why?

He passes the cigarette to her.

End of Scene 8.

Scene 9 **My Body**

Scene 9   My Body

Time: an evening several years ago

Place: a private room in a massage parlour in Chang'an, Dongguan

Characters: **Li Ke**, **Qin Yun**

Following immediately from the previous scene.

The stage is dim. **Qin Yun** *is giving* **Li Ke** *a massage in bed in a revealing work outfit.*

Ke   Why?

She ignores him.

Outside, practised greetings from the receptionists drift faintly into the room, accompanied by the chorus of responses from the female staff.

Off stage: 'Welcome sir a gentleman coming upstairs please – '

She turns him over.

Yun *(in Mandarin)*   Relax.

She holds his head and twists his neck twice. Her movements fluid and well-practised.

Yun *(in Mandarin)*   Done.

She tears open a condom.

Yun *(in Mandarin)*   Strip.

He grabs her hand.

Ke   Did you hear me? Why?

Off stage: 'Please take all your belongings sir we hope to see you again soon thanks for coming – !'

She tries to shake him off, but his grip is tight.

Yun *(in Mandarin)*   Let go of me!

Ke   Why?

Pause.

Yun   I should ask you.

Pause.

Yun   Why do you still come here?

He lets go.

She walks to the window and lights a cigarette.

Yun   Answer me.

Ke   …

Yun   I haven't got much time.

Off stage: 'Number 38! Number 38, time.'

Yun *(loudly in Mandarin)*   Yes! Almost there!

Pause.

Yun   I don't care if you want to come. Why do you have to ask for me?

Ke   …

Yun   What do you want?

Ke   To see you, to talk –

Yun   And?

Pause.

Yun   No 'and'?

Pause.

Yun   And you pay me.

Pause.

Yun   And I go to the next room and work.

Pause.

Yun   Work until the sun comes out.

Pause.

Yun   And you go back to Hong Kong.

Pause.

Yun   Right?

Ke   You can come –

Yun   No.

Ke   You can work there too.

She turns around and glares at him.

Yun *(in Mandarin)*   I never want to go to that shithole Hong Kong ever again. Do you hear me?

Ke   Why do you hate me so much?

Yun *(in Mandarin)*   I've never ever hated anyone so much.

Ke   What have I done?

Yun *(in Mandarin)*   Give me my ID back.

Ke   …

Yun *(in Mandarin)*   You hear me? Do you know how hard it is to get an ID here? –

Ke   I told you. Come to Hong Kong and I'll give it back –

Yun *(in Mandarin)*   You know I'm living in fear everyday? When I see the police walking down the streets, my hands won't stop shaking!

Ke   Why do you want to see your brother?

Yun *(in Mandarin)*   Fine, I don't want that ID. Since you like taking my things so much…

She takes her exit-entry permit for Hong Kong from her bag and throws it on the floor.

Yun *(in Mandarin)*   Here! The exit-entry permit for Hong Kong! Free with the massage!

Ke   Hey, I don't want this.

Yun *(in Mandarin)*   You see this room? I can jump I can run I can do cartwheel here! I can even smoke! I can open this window and jump out and I can even shout, aaahhh – !!! I can understand what everyone's saying and no one can scam me here!

Ke *(in Mandarin)*   You can smoke at mine –

Yun *(with a sudden gentleness in Mandarin)*   Can I stay at yours forever?

Silence.

Yun   I'm expecting.

Pause.

He looks at the cigarette in her hand.

Ke   What are you going to do?

Yun   Have it.

Ke   You're joking.

Pause.

Ke   You think this will tie him down / so you've got someone for life?

Yun *(rapidly)*   I like kids, can't you understand? *(In Mandarin)* I want a family I want my own family!

Silence.

Yun   You?

Ke   …

Yun   You… you know what you're doing?

Ke   …

Yun   You've said… I'm stunning, yeah?

Ke   …

Yun   But you haven't seen enough of me haven't seen through me, yeah?

Ke   …

Yun   You've always been curious. You always want to know why I want the lights off, yeah?

Ke   …

She takes off her clothes, holding them in one hand and gazing at him.

'Click', she turns on the lights.

Her sides, her stomach, her back seem to be covered in marks.

A relatively long

Silence.

Yun *(in Mandarin)*   This is me.

Ke   …

Yun *(in Mandarin)*   I can't change myself.

Ke   …

Yun *(in Mandarin)*   Have you seen enough?

Ke   …

Yun *(in Mandarin)*   Anything else you want to say?

End of Scene 9.

Scene 10 Night Wandering

Scene 10   Night Wandering

The **Boy** *alone.*

Boy   Curiosity is a man's strength, but being too curious can be his death.

Pause.

Boy   I'm an ordinary boy from an ordinary home. I always thought that this was an ordinary world. Being honest, reliable, moral, self-improving, speak better Mandarin… these are the things I want in this ordinary life. I could've spent my youth in an ordinary, peaceful, common way.

Pause.

Boy   But I'm too curious…

The narrator turns into the **Man**.

The **Man** *alone.*

Man   That winter on New Year's eve, I go up to Lan Kwai Fang for a couple of drinks. Lots of people are there for the countdown. Totally heaving. Of all the fun things to do in this world, countdown is definitely one of the most stupidly pointless. But I'm a pointless man, so here I am, hoping that when it turns midnight some white chick will launch herself at me and give me a big wet snog. Turns out I couldn't even get any booze and end up stuck in that sea of people on Lan Kwai for half an hour before I manage to squeeze my way out. I walk along the tram track all the way to Shau Kei

186

Wan. On the way I can't stop thinking how fucking pointless life is. Be proactive, confident, have a steady job and a stable income, be loving, filial, find a reliable woman, buy a flat, pump out a kid, bring it up... I can foresee everything. But a voice inside me is saying he's really pissed off – I don't know what – probably just too normal. Too, too normal. I need some... unusual... stimulation. That's right. Stimulation. Adventure. I'm really curious. Can I still change? As a so-called good kid, what can I change into... I'm really, really curious. So very curious. Unbearably curious.

So I...

End of Scene 10.

Scene 11 **Questions**

Scene 11   Questions

Time: early hours on New Year's day many years ago

Place: an old tong lau building

Characters: **Boy**, **Wang Jing**

Quiet singing.

Wang Jing, *she stands in the same place and holds the same pose as* **Qin Yun** *in Scene 9.*

'Click' she turns on the lights. She pauses to look at the CCTV feed.

She starts to dress but grazes a wound. The pain causes her to moan lightly.

The **Boy** *circles outside her door in hesitation.*

The door opens, startling him. She looks at him intently.

Pause.

Jing   Come in.

Pause.

He walks in, looking around.

Boy   What's that?

Jing   *CCTV.*

Boy   You can see me?

Jing   Yes, you've been filmed.

Pause.

Boy   You understand Cantonese.

Jing   Just about.

Pause.

Boy   How come you're still awake at three?

Jing   Waiting for you.

She helps him undress.

Boy   What're you doing?

Jing   Don't you know what you're here for?

Boy   …

Jing   Take a shower. Right, you can take your own clothes off.

Boy   Wah! That's a massive lizard!

Jing   Huh?

He points at the ceiling.

Jing   Oh, Xiaobai.

Boy   Xiaobai? You've given it a name?

Jing   It's a house gecko –

Boy   Gecko?

Jing   Yes, that's what you call them.

Boy   How come it's so fat?

Jing   He's been eating lots of mozzies for me. Haven't you, Xiaobai?

Boy   Get rid of it.

She ignores him and starts to undress.

Boy   What're you doing?

Jing   Again? Shower.

Boy   Oh.

Jing   You don't like this?

Boy   No.

Pause.

Jing   Strip then!

Boy   Can you make it go away?

She grabs a net and gives it to him.

Jing   Go on, big man.

He hesitates and jumps onto the bed.

She leans against the wall.

He tries to catch the gecko. Whenever he lifts his hand, the gecko shoots away.

Jing   If you hurt him, you'll have to pay.

His eyes follow the gecko's rapid movements around the room. Eventually he turns round and ends up looking at her.

She claps and the gecko runs into the wardrobe.

Boy   … in the wardrobe.

Jing   Happy now?

She takes his trousers off. He quickly covers himself up with the net.

She pulls him into the bathroom.

Chattering and the sound of the shower drift in from the bathroom.

Jing   Turn around.

Boy   Eh?

Jing   Turn around. How do I wash your willy when you keep sticking your bum at me?

Boy   Oh.

Jing   You've got decent skin.

Boy   Your neck's bruised.

Jing   …

Boy *(frightened)*   Oi… what're you doing?

Jing   Not again! Helping you wash.

Boy   Oi… oi!

Jing   Open your mouth.

Boy   What for?

Jing   Mouthwash.

He takes a swig of the mouthwash.

Jing   Back here. Here. Needs to be washed often, clear?

She scrubs hard. He moans.

Boy   I've swallowed it.

Jing   All right. Turn around. Turn. March! Sit outside and wait.

He comes out wrapped in a towel and sits on the bed.

He picks up a piece of silk at the head of the bed. A needle and some threads are sticking out.

She is humming the song "Liuyang River" in the bathroom.

She walks towards the bed also wrapped in a towel.

Jing   Looks nice, eh?

Boy   What is it?

Jing   Cross stitch.

He puts it down.

Boy   Sit.

She sits. He puts his arm around her shoulders.

Boy   What's your name?

Jing   My, my, you've changed.

He pulls his arm away.

Pause.

Jing   Benz.

Boy   Huh?

Jing   Never heard that?

Boy   Benz? It's a car.

Jing   Yes, not everyone can afford it.

He grabs her breast.

Boy *(in Mandarin)*   Then I'm so lucky.

She moans in pain.

Boy   What's wrong?

She shakes her head.

Jing   Come, lie down. Be good.

Boy   Oh.

Pause.

Boy   How long have you been doing this?

Pause.

Jing   Couple of months.

Pause.

Jing   Haven't you got a girlfriend?

Boy   Wouldn't be here if I'd got one.

Jing   Get one then.

Boy   Cost too much.

Jing   Huh?

Boy   Dating costs.

Jing   Don't do this often?

Boy   First time.

Jing   Oh – you're doing this at your age, what's going to happen when you get old?

Boy   I've never done it.

Pause.

Jing   Eh?

Boy *(in Mandarin)*   I'm a virgin.

Pause.

She looks at him intently.

Jing   Yeah right.

Boy *(in Mandarin)*   Really.

Pause.

Boy *(in Mandarin)*   You've got to believe me.

Silence.

Jing   What're we going to do with you?

Boy   What? It's nothing.

Jing   Don't blame me.

She tears open a condom.

Boy   What're you doing?

Jing   Get you up.

Pause.

Boy   Do I have to? *(In Mandarin)* I'm clean.

Pause.

Jing   Fine. Only this once.

She goes down.

Jing   You're shivering.

Boy   I'm a bit cold.

She puts a blanket on his stomach and heads back down.

Jing   Let me go. I can't blow with you grabbing my head.

A minute later.

Jing   Nearly there. I'll lie down and you come in?

Boy   I don't know how…

Jing   Fine. I'll do it. You'll have to wear this.

Boy   Uh-huh.

She takes out a condom.

A moment.

She starts to ease herself on him.

Boy   Hang on… slower…

Jing   What's wrong? Not comfy?

Boy   Uh-huh, a little.

She moves.

Boy   Oi, hang on, hang on…

She stops.

Boy   Hurts a bit…

Jing   The first time always feels a bit odd.

Boy   Slower… slower…

They stop.

Jing   You're soft.

Boy   Sorry.

She gets up and goes down again.

A minute later, she tears open another condom and puts it on.

Jing   Right, quick.

Boy   Slower! …

She speeds up.

Boy   Slower!

She slows down.

Silence.

Jing   Not again.

Boy   Sorry.

Jing   You don't have to…

Boy   Sorry.

Jing   Dear me, you're working me hard…

She goes down again.

Boy   I'll try harder.

A moment later, she lifts her head.

Jing   I'll lie down, you do it. Quick.

Boy   Oh.

He fumbles around.

Jing   What're you doing?

Boy   How?

Jing   Give it to me.

Boy   …

More fumbling.

Jing   Soft again.

He sits on the bed.

Silence.

Boy   Seems like… I don't feel it.

Jing   For me?

Boy   No, no. It's my problem…

Pause.

Jing   Hm, what should we do?

Silence.

She kisses him.

After a while, she straddles him in one swift, practised move.

A moment.

Boy   Hang on, hang on…

Jing   Hush, or you'll go soft again.

Boy   No, no…

She ignores him.

Boy   Really, no…

Jing   What now?

Boy   Xiaobai is coming at me!

Jing   …

Boy   It's almost on my head!

Jing   Hold a little longer!

Boy   Oi! Oi!

End of Scene 11.

Scene 12 **A Song from Home**

Scene 12   A Song from Home

Time: same as previous scene

Place: same as previous scene

Characters: same as previous scene

*The **Boy** is lying on **Wang Jing** and she is holding him.*

A moment later, he rolls over. They look tired.

At the start of the scene, it is still dark outside. Gradually, by the end, the day has dawned.

Jing   Almost dawn.

Pause.

Jing   Phew… one of you is like taking 10 in a go.

Boy   … sorry.

Jing   Not bad for your first time. Can you do it again?

Pause.

Boy   Don't do this to me.

Pause.

Boy   That… Xiaobai?

Jing   He's full and sleeping.

Boy   Oh, did I completely overrun…

Jing   Doesn't matter. It's been a quiet day. I've done three cross stitches already.

Boy   Sorry –

Jing   Told you not to say sorry again –

Boy   Sor…

Pause.

He picks up the piece of silk by the bed.

Boy   What're you making?

Jing   Flowers.

Boy   Doesn't look like it.

Jing   Fireworks flowers.

Pause.

Boy   You like sewing?

Jing   I'm bored. This can kill time.

Boy   Who's this for?

Jing   My daughter.

Pause.

Jing   Do you mind if I smoke?

He nods.

She lights up.

Jing   Want some?

He shakes his head.

Jing   C'mon, to celebrate your first time.

Boy   Don't know how.

Jing   I'll teach you.

She puts the cigarette in his mouth.

Jing   Inhale a little into your mouth… then, just like you're breathing in fresh air…

She shows him how to inhale deeply.

He tries to emulate but ends up choking.

She pats his back with a laugh and gives him some water.

Silence.

Jing   Is this really your first time?

Boy   Yeah.

She opens the drawer next to the bed and pulls out a red envelope.

Jing   All the best.

Pause.

Boy   I haven't even paid you.

Jing   Take this.

Pause.

Boy   Thank you!

Jing   Don't be so happy! It's only a dollar!

Silence.

He wants to try smoking the cigarette in his hand.

She gives him an ashtray.

Jing   Don't smoke the last third.

They lie side by side in bed, looking at the ceiling.

Boy   What were you singing in the shower?

Jing   A song from home.

Boy   Where's your home?

Jing   Hunan. You know where that is?

Boy   Yeah, up north.

Jing   Let me tell you Hong Kong lot again. Hunan is in the south. Only north of the Yangtze is the north.

Boy Oh...

Pause.

Boy Yangtze and the Yellow River... what's their relationship?

Jing Both are water.

Pause.

Boy What's your hometown famous for?

Jing Fireworks. Liuyang's fireworks are the most famous.

Boy And?

Jing Liuyang River.

Boy River? Is it pretty?

Jing Don't know. Haven't been back for ages.

Pause.

Jing It's been a long time.

Pause.

Jing I heard it's turning into an open sewer.

Pause.

Boy Why don't you go back?

Jing I can't.

Boy Aren't you bored stuck in this room all day? There's no light at all.

Jing (*smiles*) I've got Xiaobai.

Boy You should get rid of these things on the window. I'll help you –

Jing No, the sun is really strong in the morning –

Boy Sun?

Jing   Uh-huh.

Boy   You can see the sun here?

Jing   And sunrise too.

Boy   What?

Jing   Sunrise –

Boy   You're kidding.

Jing   See that really tall building?

Boy   They're everywhere – which one?

Jing   There. HSBC in giant letters. The sun rises there.

Boy   You sure?

Jing   There's a piece of glass. It reflects the sun straight into here.

Boy   Really?

Jing   When the sun rises, it's like it's on fire in here. Bright red!

Boy   Can't believe you can see the sunrise here.

Jing   For five minutes every day. Right… about now!

The room begins to glow red. It's getting brighter.

A long silence. A bird or two chirps intermittently.

Boy   When will you go back to Hunan?

Jing   …

Boy   You won't go back?

Jing   …

Boy   Why?

Jing   …

Boy   Won't your family be waiting?

Jing   …

Boy   Don't you miss them?

Pause.

Boy   Can you sing again?

Jing   What?

Boy   The song just now.

Pause.

She starts singing "Liuyang River".

Jing   *Liuyang River*

How many bends are there?

How long until it meets the Xiang River?

What's that town on the bank?

Who's that famous figure from this place?

Leading the people to liberation

Aa-yi-aa-yi-zi-yo

Liuyang River

After you pass nine bends

The Xiang River is 50 miles away

On the bank is Xiangtan town

…

The room seems to be on fire. Its warmth is intoxicating.

Boy   What's your name?

Jing   Wang Jing.

End of Scene 12.

Scene 13 **Foreign Land**

Scene 13　Foreign Land

Li Ke *alone.*

Ke　Wang Jing. The first time I hear the name. A pool of spring water appears in front of me – quiet, peaceful, glittering, beautiful.

So I jump in and dive to the bottom.

A coolness permeates my skin. The wavering sunlight grazes my brow. I spot a tram, so I swim aboard and grab a window seat. The tram totters along and onto Wanchai. It totters on, into the Harbour. It keeps on tottering, onto Kowloon. I can see in an alleyway a woman inhaling deeply. Then she chucks an unfinished cigarette down the drain. Rings of smoke drift towards a window, where a kid is leaning, staring wide-eyed at his Mickey Mouse balloon flying into the air. Mickey flies to the rooftop of a building, where there's a green bamboo forest. In the distance, a bunch of men in yellow hats climb up and down, traversing with ease. All of a sudden, just in front of me, a shoal of fish wearing orange tops flit back and forth. I reach out. They kiss my palm, the back of my hand, my fingers, like a dragonfly gliding over water. I blink and they're all gone, flitting somewhere just below the window. So I look down, I can see the whole of Hong Kong. Wanchai, the Harbour, Kowloon, the New Territories… Like a piece of silk blowing in the wind. It's spotted with tiny black images. Oh, it's actually a forest. A forest as wide and deep as the sea. New Year, the start of a new year – I've changed so much that I don't know this world anymore.

End of Scene 13.

Scene 14 **Breaking the Ice**

Scene 14   Breaking the Ice

Time: back to Scene 1

Place: the **Man**'s *flat*

Characters: **Man**, **Girl**

The **Girl's** *laughter is accompanied by the sound of rain outside.*

She is half-drunk, with a cigarette dangling from her lips. She is twisting the Rubik's Cube frantically and without strategy.

The **Man** *has nearly completed his model.*

Girl   That's so sad.

Man   …

Girl   So sad. So, so sad. Ha ha. Are all of you housebound nerds… no need to feel sorry. Don't feel sorry. I'll give you some love.

Pause.

Man   Oh.

Girl   Ha, so sad. But it's different now. There are many more choices.

Man   How?

Girl   Lots. We put in feelings, effort!

Man   Oh.

Girl   How old were you?

Man   19.

Girl   Ha.

Man   What?

Girl   I'm way ahead.

Man   You?

Pause.

Girl   14.

Pause.

Girl   Call me big sis.

Man   Big sis.

Girl   Ha.

Man   You seem like a real pro.

Girl   To date I've been in three, four, five… seven, no, eight! Eight relationships.

Man   Young achiever.

Girl   You really need warmth…

Man   …

Girl   So sad. So, so sad. Why don't I warm you up?

Man   What did it feel like at 14?

Pause.

Man   Losing it at 14.

Girl   What?

Pause.

Girl   Nothing special. Wanted to try so tried it…

Man   How long were you together for?

Girl   …

Man   A month?

Girl   Can't remember.

Man   A week?

Girl   …

Man   Oh…

Girl   …

Pause.

Man   Wang Jing has a daughter. Xiaorou. She went to Taipei with her dad. I went to see her. She gave me this model. See, it can be made into different things.

Girl   Ha ha ha. You and Wang Jing… still going?

Man   I took a few pictures of Xiaorou. She asked me if I'd seen her mum.

Pause.

Man   I said, *(in Mandarin)* 'Yes. There's this thing internet these days. It's easy to see people.' Then she took out this model and said, *(in Mandarin)* 'Mum said she'd come for me once she's got a house. Get her this internet thing and tell her to come soon!'

Girl   Ha ha, she's so cute.

Man   Yeah. You should get one!

Girl   Ha ha, what about tonight?

Man   God, you're keen.

Girl   What about Qin Yun?

Man   Eh?

Girl   Haha, has she got one? Did she pump one out?

Man   Yeah.

Girl   Ha ha ha!

Man   Ha ha ha!

Girl   She must've heard your story and thinks kids are cute!

Man   Ha ha, yeah, yeah!

He looks at her intently.

She pours a bowl of vodka.

Man   Shouldn't drink so much.

Girl   I can hold it.

Man   You've drunk a few hundred already.

Girl   If that's what I want, that's what I do! OK? Ha ha! Let's get back to the point. Are you talking so much so you can shag me? Are you thinking of pulling me so you can save –

Man   Is this how you lost it – the first time?

Pause.

She slams the bowl on the table, spilling everywhere.

Girl   Is this a game?

Man   …

Girl   You think I'm fun to toy with?

Man   …

Girl   I can play with you.

Man   …

Girl   I know the game.

Man   You need someone to love –

Girl   Thanks but no thanks, all right?

Man   You've drunk too much.

Girl   I know full well what I want.

Man   What do you want? –

Girl   Dignity. You?

Man   …

Girl   Have you got any?

Man   …

Girl   I can say no to my clients.

Man   …

Girl   Everything I've got, I've earned myself.

Man   …

Girl   You?

Man   …

Girl   How dare you talk to me with that look in your eyes?

Man   What look? –

Girl   I don't need anything, / I only need respect. Do you know what respect is?

Man   I'm asking you, what look?

Girl   Don't think you're Casanova just 'cause you've slept with a few tarts. You're just a wee John. Real cheap. You're fooling around since the start. What gives you the rights to pity me?

Pause.

Man   You think I pity you? –

Girl   And you look down on me.

Man   Look down?

Girl   Isn't that why you're telling me all that?!

Man   What's wrong with that? –

Girl   You made a point of telling me all that!

Man   Made a point?

Girl   The way you talk about them is like you're talking about me!

Pause.

Man   Don't get carried away –

Girl   I'm not –

Man   I'm not talking about you.

Girl   …

Man   I'm… talking about myself.

Girl   …

Man   You told me to talk about it.

Girl   I did?

Man   On WeChat that time, you said you know what I'm talking about.

Girl   …

Man   I just want a friend –

Girl   Friend? You got me here just to 'make friends'?!

Man   This is not what you think –

Girl   What do you think this is then?

Man   I don't think anything.

Girl   Why am I sitting here listening to all your fucking shit?! –

Man   I've paid already. Get that right?! –

Girl   What? –

Man   I've paid! You have to satisfy me!

Girl   That's compensated dating! –

Man   I'll say it again! It's not!

Girl   Then what is it?

Man   Compensated dating is really cheap!

Silence. Slightly longer than usual.

Girl   Oh, do you know what sort of man are you?

She lights up.

Girl   Do you really think you understand your Qin Yun, your Wang Jing, your thingamy?

Pause.

Girl   Do you really think you miss them? You pity them? You're grateful to them?

Pause.

Girl   Then why don't you do anything?

Man   I –

Girl   Why can't you face it?

Pause.

Man   Face what?

Girl   Your hypocrisy.

She whips her trousers off and opens her legs wide. She takes a drag of the cigarette and stares at him.

Girl   Come on.

Black out. The only light is the glow of the cigarette.

End of Scene 14.

Scene 15 **Elopement**

Scene 15   Elopement

Time: late at night on the eve of Chinese New Year, many years ago

Place: a park in Tin Shui Wai

Characters: **Wang Jing**, **Boy**

Complete darkness. The only light is the glow of the cigarette. It's moving slowly.

An empty park. There's a stone staircase going up.

Boy   Come on.

*A spot of flickering light, it's **Wang Jing** lighting her lighter.*

Jing   It's pitch black. What kinda hellhole is this?

Boy   A park. No one comes here at this time. Come sit.

She sits on the steps. He tries to empty his trousers pockets.

She gives him some light.

Boy   Want some chocolate?

Jing   …

Boy   Sweets?

Jing   …

Boy   Biscuits?

Jing   …

Boy   Egg tart? Bun?

Jing   …

Boy   That's all I've got. It's not easy to get them out. If you didn't know, you'd think I was going to pay tribute to some god.

Jing   Lordy, all from your pockets. Still hot, right?

Boy   …

She flicks off the lighter.

Jing   We haven't met for a year, eh?

Boy   You remember?

Jing   …

Boy   Why have you been ignoring my calls in the last few months?

Jing   I've told you already. He's keeping a tight watch.

Boy   That rich kid?

Pause.

Jing   Why aren't you spending time with your parents tonight? It's Chinese New Year.

Boy   Who said they'd come all the way to Tin Shui Wai to see me?

Jing   I haven't got anywhere else to go.

Boy   It's three in the morning. You're just like Xiaobai – a night creature.

She throws her cigarette away.

Jing   Go home then.

Pause.

Boy   Hungry? –

He pulls out a chicken leg and passes it to her.

Jing   Thanks.

She munches on it.

Boy   Is Xiaorou all right?

Pause.

She nods.

Boy   Xiaobai? How's it doing?

Jing   Snuffed it.

Boy   Gone?

Jing   Still stuck on the window.

Boy   How?

Jing   The sun. Sundried, like a salted fish.

Pause.

Jing   That time you helped me take the things off the window and put up some curtains. There was still a bit of sticky stuff left on the window. Xiaobai got stuck.

Boy   How come he was there?

Jing   Lots of mozzies were stuck.

Boy   …

Jing   His tail was torn. He clearly struggled.

Boy   You didn't notice?

Jing   No, I was on holiday for a week.

Pause.

Boy   With that rich kid? –

Jing   Oh, I'm so full.

She throws the bone into the distance and wipes her hand.

Jing   Happy.

Pause.

Jing   I'm so happy.

Pause.

Jing   You know, Hong Kong is a carefree place.

Boy   Yeah?

Jing   It doesn't require thinking.

Boy   Eh?

Jing   'Cause people here are just like you…

Boy   What?

Jing   Brainless! Ha ha!

She runs up a couple of steps and stops at the top.

Boy   Oi, careful. It's dark, don't fall over!

Jing   Wow, you can see the lights here!

He follows her to the top.

Jing   Hey – ! Hong – Kong – ! I – love – you – !

Boy   She can't understand Mandarin!

Jing   Teach me Cantonese then.

Boy   She doesn't like Canto.

Jing   What does she like then?

Boy   Honkie Chinglish!

Jing   Hong Kong I love u! –

Boy   You missed out the 'ar'. Without the 'ar', it's not Honkie. After me: Hong Kong I luf u ar!

Jing   Hong Kong I love u ar!

Boy   Don't need to say 'love' so clearly: Hong Kong I luf u ar!

Jing   Hong Kong I love u ar!

Boy   Got it!

Jing   Hong Kong I love u ar! Hong Kong I love u ar! Hong Kong I love u ar.

Pause.

He takes out a sparkler.

Boy   Want some?

Jing   Oh, sparklers?

Boy   I'll take you somewhere safe to light this.

Jing   Ah ha, what luck! I've got some too!

She takes out a small box of fireworks.

Boy   Coconuts?!

Jing   Happy?

Boy   You've got coconuts that big?!

Jing   Shall we set some off?

Boy   These make a racket. Where did you get them?

Jing   A colleague brought it from Liuyang. Have you forgotten? It's my hometown speciality.

Boy   No, no. We can't set those grenades off.

Jing *(sternly)*   We have to set fireworks off to celebrate Chinese new year.

Boy *(sternly)*   No way. I don't want to go to jail –

Jing   Fine.

Pause.

Jing   You're a spoilsport.

Pause.

Boy   Sorry.

Pause.

She takes a photograph from her wallet.

Jing   This is me five years ago.

Boy   …

Jing   Changed lots, eh?

Boy   Yeah?

Jing   Oh.

Pause.

Jing   I'm old.

Pause.

Jing   Not as good-looking as before.

Pause.

Jing   Don't tell me you can't tell that I'm 30-something, *(in Cantonese)* kiddo.

Boy   …

Jing   Can't you see the wrinkles around my eyes? I'm already a mother.

Boy   …

Jing   My breasts are sagging.

Boy   …

Jing   But I'm still a bit of a looker, eh?

Boy   …

She hugs him from behind.

Jing   Women are like fireworks.

Pause.

Jing 'Puff!' That's it.

Pause.

Jing Gone.

Pause.

Jing Take a couple of pictures with me?

Boy …

Jing I'm leaving in the morning, boy.

Boy Where?

Jing Canada.

Boy Oh, he's going to Canada?

Jing Yeah, they think Hong Kong's done.

Boy You're going to stay with him?

Jing …

Boy So everything I've said was wasted.

Pause.

Boy I said you need to be –

Jing Independent –

Boy Yeah.

Pause.

Boy You can. Be brave –

Jing I can't.

Boy You just don't want to. You're used to this / kind of life.

Jing Yes. I don't have a choice. You want me to get a proper job and earn a couple of grand a month and bring up a six-year-old kid? –

Boy   Nothing's going to happen between you two. He's so young. He just wanted something new. He's going to ditch you sooner or later! –

Jing   So?

Boy   Leave him.

Pause.

Jing   What you just said, why didn't you say it a year ago?

Boy   …

Jing   A year ago when I told you I'm getting together with him why / didn't you make a sound?

Boy   I can't do anything to help you –

Jing   Did I want anything from you?

Boy   …

Jing   Now I've got no choices and you're telling me to leave him?

Boy   …

Jing   Why do you men only ever speak up when I've run out of options? –

Boy   You wanted to have the girl. You said you'll use her to tie the father down –

Jing   No one told me I can't tie him down. Now I don't even have a daughter.

Pause.

Boy   Where's she now?

Jing   He went to Hunan and took her to Taiwan.

Boy   …

Jing   Phew, now I'm sorta free. I can go where I like.

Boy   I can go find her for you.

Jing   Ha ha, you want to help me?

Boy   I can.

Jing   Ha ha.

Boy   You don't believe me?

Jing   You really want to help me?

Boy   …

Jing   Then just watch from afar.

Pause.

Jing   Like watching fireworks.

She takes her camera out and gives it to him.

Jing   Take a few pictures.

Boy   …

Jing   With the flash. Further away. All the way to the bottom.

Boy   …

Jing   Go.

Boy   It's dark as hell. How can I see where you are?

She lights a cigarette.

Jing   Now you can. Just point at this.

Boy   Oh.

Jing   Wait.

She puts the cigarette in his mouth. She lights another one.

Boy   You know I don't smoke.

Jing   Keep it there, so I know how far you've gone.

He takes the camera and walks a couple of steps away.

Jing Further! Bit more! You need to get the steps in. And the tree. That's right. There, there. That's the spot!

She waves her cigarette.

Jing Hey! Can you see me?

Boy Yeah!

She lights a sparkler with her cigarette. He notices.

Boy Oi! Not here!

Jing Take it now!

Pause.

Jing It's almost gone. I'm lighting another one.

Boy All right, all right.

He takes a few photographs. The flash goes off a few times.

The sparkler burns itself out.

Complete darkness.

Boy Hey! It's gone!

Pause.

Jing We've got more!

She lights up one of the coconut fireworks.

A shooting star cuts through the dark sky and blooms.

The sparks illuminate everything. The **Boy** *vanishes and turns into* **Li Ke***.*

Complete darkness.

A second shooting star. Its sparks once again illuminating everything. **Li Ke** *becomes the* **Man.**

Time seems to have sunk into the sea. Everything is 10 times slower.

Jing Hey – !

Man   Hey – !

Jing   The sky is blooming – !

Ke   We'll be locked up tomorrow – !

Jing   Make a wish – !

Boy   Huh – !

Jing   Shooting star – !

Man   What – ?!

Jing   Shooting stars everywhere – !

Ke   Where are you going – !

Jing   I want to see them clearer – !

She looks up into the night sky. She seems to elevate, rising from the surface of the earth.

Boy   I'm here to help you – !

Jing   Don't come over – !

Ke   Can't you stay – ?!

Jing   You don't need to come over – !

Man   I know – !

Jing   If you come over, there'd be no other way – !

Boy   I've got one – !

Jing   Really – ?!

Ke   I don't – !

Jing   Then just look after my flowers – !

Man   What flowers – ?!

*She throws a long roll of white silk, it flies towards the **Boy**.*

Jing The shooting star flowers I embroidered – ! Don't they look just right – ?!

The white silk unfurls slowly. It's translucently thin. There's no pattern. It rises gradually, filling the whole night sky.

Jing 10 a day, more than 3,000 flowers – !

Boy …

Jing All yours – !

Ke …

Jing The nights in Hong Kong are long – !

Man …

Jing Day and night I've been thinking, when will I ever see the shooting stars bloom – !

Boy …

Jing They really are real – !

Her feet lift off the ground.

Boy Don't move – !

Jing Shooting stars can bloom – !

Ke It's just flowers – !

Jing They bloom…

Boy What's so special – ?!

Jing Then they bear fruit – !

Ke Stop looking – !

Jing I want to see that – !

Boy They don't matter – !

Jing I want to – !

Ke   What if you can't – ?!

Jing   I want to see clearer – !

Boy   Don't go further – !

Jing   Such beautiful flowers…

Ke   Can't save you – !

Jing   What fruit will they bear – ?!

The **Man** *leaps forward to the top of the stairs, holding onto her legs tightly.*

Man   None! Nothing! Don't you understand? Nothing. Nothing. Can't you fucking understand? Don't go. Don't go further. I can't anymore. I've done everything. If I don't say it now, I'll die. I really will. I've been going to them all year. During the day. At night. Whenever I've got a moment. But I'm not happy with any of them. Not a single one I'm happy with. I do it… no, I shag them. Then I pay. 'No, this is not what I want, not what I want.' Every time I'm done, that's how I feel. I try to trick myself, but the voice won't bloody go away! 'Not what I want, not what I want.' Each time it just digs further into the wound. But I just don't have the guts to admit that I've no balls, no use and no shame. I don't know how I turned into this cunt face. I've never felt so despicable, so hypocritical, so fake. I really want to die. Death will make it so fucking much better! I keep thinking, how much longer do I have to stay in this hell… until a moment ago when you held me, just like how I'm holding you now.

End of Scene 15.

Scene 16 **A Cigarette**

Scene 16 A Cigarette

Darkness.

A match is struck.

A cigarette appears. Someone takes a long drag. It glows weakly in the dark.

(In Cantonese) He lights a cigarette. Silky white smoke meanders mid-air. His eyes flit and dart in this haze. This caressing trace curls around his waist, lifting him out of the window, drifting towards that sleepy sky. He gently pushes the fluffy clouds apart, swimming towards the flickering stars. Only then does he realise, on that other side of the sky, there are countless like him. They each stand on their own little planet – in a daze, in deep thought, anxious… and they all happen to have a cigarette in their hand. Some would take a long drag, so in that dark night, a short but brief glow would cut through. Some would puff lightly, so in the distance there are weak but continuous spots of starlight. Dotted here and there, far and close, planets after planets separated by who knows how many light years. They are there, waiting, but they'll never reach each other. They are cigarettes that never burn out, they are cigarettes that can never be finished.

(In Cantonese) He's no longer lonely, gazing at the twinkling sky. But he is alone. He has no choice but to light up, to send a weak signal to the distant distance. Perhaps, everyone will inhale deeply at the same time. So in that moment of deep loneliness, the sky will be illuminated and darkness expelled.

Alas, we can't see each other's signal, we can't synchronise. The only thing left to do is to inhale this whole long night of solitude into our chest, and hope that before dawn, we can exhale enough to form a cloud to shield us from the heat.

End of Scene 16.

Scene 17 Metamorphosis

Scene 17   Metamorphosis

Time: back to Scene 1, five in the morning

Place: the **Man***'s flat*

Characters: **Boy**, **Girl**

The rain has stopped. There is an occasional drip falling on the window.

The **Girl** *alone. She is sitting on the bed, putting make up on. There is a 1,000-dollar note on the coffee table.*

The **Boy** *comes out of the bathroom, drying his hair with a towel.*

He then starts blow-drying it.

She packs up her things.

He turns on the stereo, Coldplay's "Yellow" is playing quietly.

He pours a glass of water, sits on the bed and gives it to her.

Girl   It's all right.

Pause.

Girl   It was raining hard last night.

Boy   Yeah.

Pause.

Boy   Sorry.

Girl   Huh?

Boy   I've overrun…

Girl   Oh, I thought it would anyway.

Pause.

Girl   Do you think Hong Kong would be flooded?

Boy   …

Girl   If it is, I bet everyone will be fucking joyous.

Boy   …

Girl   The MTR'd stop. The buses cancelled. The border closed. That shop at the junction run by the Chows would be closed. None of those mainlanders can barge in and buy up all the gold. Everyone in Hong Kong can float around on their big yellow duckies, faff around on boats…

She's done packing.

Girl   I'm going.

Boy   Oh…

Pause.

Boy   Right…

He gives her back her watch.

Pause.

She takes it.

Pause.

She takes out the Rubik's Cube.

Girl   I've done it…

He tries to take it but she won't let go.

Girl   Did anyone say you're longwinded?

Boy   Eh?

Girl   You… talk so fucking much.

Boy   Oh.

Pause.

Boy   Maybe 'cause I haven't spoken for too long.

Girl   Too long?

Boy   Yeah… quite long… it's been.

Pause.

She gives him the Rubik's Cube.

Girl   Actually I remember.

Boy   What?

Girl   That we've talked lots before this…

Boy   Oh…

Girl   But… we've never met… was a bit nervous…

Pause.

Girl   I'll tell you a secret.

Boy   Huh?

She leans over and whispers in his ear.

He stares at her.

Pause.

Boy   Yeah right.

Girl *(in Mandarin)*   It's true.

Pause.

Girl *(in Mandarin)*   You must believe me.

Pause.

Boy   Ha.

Girl   Ha ha.

Birds chirp intermittently.

Girl Even the birds are singing, ha ha.

She opens a window. It's the ocean.

She inhales deeply.

Pause.

Girl Good morning, Hong Kong.

Boy Morning…

Girl Good morning, Hong Kong!

All kinds of echo return.

In a distance, there are people rowing and swimming.

Girl How long do you think it'll take to swim to Tin Shui Wai?

Boy Two… three hours?

Girl Ha, even if I get there I probably can't get myself onto dry land.

Pause.

Boy Got any change?

Girl Huh?

He puts a few coins into her hand.

Boy Get the ferry.

Girl Huh?

Boy But you'll have to swim to the pier first…

Girl …

Boy Want to me see you off?

Pause.

Girl *(in Mandarin)* Just watch from afar.

They look out of the window.

The **Man** *picks up the model house and goes to the window. He leans out to put it on the water.*

The house with the toy hippo quietly floats into the distance.

The sun rises slowly from the horizon.

Girl   What's the song about?

Boy   … eh?

Pause.

The **Boy** *explains hesitantly as he sings.*

Boy   Look at them stars…

Pause.

Boy   Look how they twink and twink…

Pause.

Boy   Twinkle away for you…

Pause.

Boy   Eh they're a bit freaked out…

Pause.

Boy   I've followed you…

Pause.

Boy   I write a song for you…

Pause.

Boy   'Bout whatever stuff you do…

Pause.

Boy   It is called freaked out…

Pause.

Boy   So then I decide…

Pause.

Boy   I want to pull you…

Pause.

Boy   But then I start…

Pause.

Boy   To freak out…

He continues.

The red morning light blazes through the window into the house, turning everything into a fiery red.

A black shadow is cast on the wall. It is shifting slowly in the red light.

It is the shadow of the gecko.

The end.

Translator's Note

This is the second play by Wang Haoran that I have translated. And I find that I am up against the same problems as before.

Problem one: dialects. Wang's characters speak either Cantonese or Mandarin, sometimes both. How do I render these two dialects with their distinct sounds and vocabulary into one language – English?

I thought of using accents. British vs American, Geordie vs Essex, for example. But I quickly ruled out that idea because it'd be incomprehensible when projected as subtitles. More importantly, the cultural and social connotations embodied in an accent are not something I wanted to bring to characters from an entirely different part of the world.

In the end, I chose to adhere to the basic rule that all playwright-translators recommend: whatever the characters say, it must be what a native English speaker would say in that particular situation. It must sound natural. This is a translation intended to be spoken out loud – acted out.

Problem two: Cantonese. It is a dialect with a limited set of standardised written representations. There are invented characters and borrowed sounds. Meaning is more reliant on exclamations, tones and stresses rather than the actual words being said. So deciphering this manuscript and understanding its nuances was all about talking to myself out loud – very loud! I hope that my interpretation does not diverge too much from our actors and director's understanding.

Problem three: culturally specific phrasing and insults. As an entirely different civilisation, Chinese reference points often don't have Judeo-Christian counterparts, the culture that the English language is rooted in. So to create credible insults and references (that would spring from the mouth of a native English speaker), I took some liberty with regards to meaning and choice of words. For example, in Cantonese, 'to get ashore' – apart from its literal meaning – implies getting sorted out for life, financially and otherwise. At the end of the play, Wang uses the phrase referring to both its literal and implied meanings. The best colloquial equivalent I could think of is 'getting your feet onto dry land'. Not quite the same, but hopefully it conveys both the meaning and the image.

I am grateful to Wang Haoran for answering my long list of questions patiently and checking the translation drafts carefully. And I am much indebted to Nathan Rippin for the many excellent suggestions and useful comments.

Gigi Chang is a writer and translator specialising in visual and performing arts. She has translated numerous Chinese operas and new plays for the Hong Kong Arts Festival, including Wang Haoran's first play *Blast* (2013).

香港藝術節
HONG KONG ARTS FESTIVAL (HKAF)

香港藝術節於 1973 年正式揭幕，是國際藝壇中重要的文化盛事，於每年 2、3 月期間呈獻約 150 場演出及約 250 項「加料」和教育節目，致力豐富香港的文化生活。

香港藝術節是一所**非牟利機構**，約三成經費來自香港特區政府的撥款、約四成來自票房收入，而餘下約三成則有賴各大企業、熱心人士及慈善基金會的贊助和捐款。

香港藝術節每年呈獻眾多**國際演藝名家**的演出，例如：芭托莉、卡里拉斯、馬友友、格拉斯、馬素爾、沙爾、巴里殊尼哥夫、紀蓮、史柏西、皇家阿姆斯特丹音樂廳樂團、聖彼得堡馬林斯基劇院基洛夫樂團及合唱團、巴伐利亞國立歌劇院、紐約市芭蕾舞團、巴黎歌劇院芭蕾舞團、翩娜．包殊烏珀塔爾舞蹈劇場、雲門舞集、星躍馬術奇藝坊、皇家莎士比亞劇團、莫斯科藝術劇院及北京人民藝術劇院等。

香港藝術節積極推介**本地演藝人才和新晉藝術家**，並**委約及製作**多套全新戲劇、室內歌劇和當代舞蹈作品，甚或出版新作劇本，不少作品已在香港及海外多度重演。

香港藝術節大力投資下一代的藝術教育。**「青少年之友」**外展計劃成立 23 年來，已為約 700,000 位本地中學生及大專生提供藝術體驗活動。藝術節每年亦通過**「學生票捐助計劃」**提供近 9,000 張半價學生票。

香港藝術節每年主辦逾百項深入社區的**加料節目**，例如示範講座、大師班、工作坊、座談會、後台參觀、展覽、藝談、導賞團等，鼓勵觀眾與藝術家互相接觸。

HKAF, launched in 1973, is a major international arts festival committed to enriching the life of the city by presenting about 150 performances and 250 PLUS and educational events in February and March every year.

HKAF is a **non-profit organisation**, with about 30% of annual revenue from government funding, around 40% from the box office, and the remaining 30% from sponsorships and donations from corporations, individuals, and charitable foundations.

HKAF presents **top international artists and ensembles**, such as Bartoli, Carreras, Yo-Yo Ma, Glass, Masur, Chailly, Baryshnikov, Guillem, Spacey, the Royal Concertgebouw Orchestra, the Mariinsky Theatre and Valery Gergiev, Bavarian State Opera, New York City Ballet, Paris Opera Ballet, Tanztheater Wuppertal Pina Bausch, Cloud Gate Dance Theatre, Zingaro, Royal Shakespeare Company, Moscow Art Theatre, and the People's Art Theatre of Beijing.

HKAF actively promotes **Hong Kong's own creative talents and emerging artists**, and **commissions, produces and publishes new works** in theatre, chamber opera and contemporary dance, many with successful subsequent runs in Hong Kong and overseas.

HKAF invests in **arts education** for young people. In the past 23 years, our **Young Friends** has reached about 700,000 secondary and tertiary school students in Hong Kong. Donations to the **Student Ticket Scheme** make available close to 9,000 half-price student tickets each year.

HKAF organises over 100 **Festival PLUS** activities in community locations each year to enhance the engagement between artists and audiences. These include lecture demonstrations, masterclasses, workshops, symposia, backstage visits, exhibitions, meet-the-artist sessions, and guided tours.

欲**贊助或捐助**香港藝術節，請與藝術節發展部聯絡。
Please contact the HKAF Development Dept for sponsorship opportunities and donation details.

電郵 Email	直線 Direct Lines	網頁 Website
dev@hkaf.org	(852) 2828 4910/11/12	www.hk.artsfestival.org/en/partner

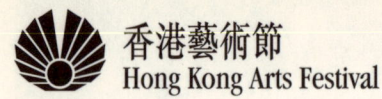

香港藝術節
Hong Kong Arts Festival

地址 Address: 香港灣仔港灣道2號12樓1205室
Room 1205, 12th Floor, 2 Harbour Road,
Wanchai, Hong Kong

電話 Tel: 傳真 Fax: 電子郵箱 Email:
2824 3555   2824 3798, 2824 3722   afgen@hkaf.org

節目查詢熱線 Programme Enquiry Hotline: 2824 2430

出版：香港藝術節協會有限公司
承印：香港嘉昱有限公司
本刊內容，未經許可，不得轉載。

Published by: Hong Kong Arts Festival Society Limited
Printed by: Cheer Shine Enterprise Co., Ltd
Reproduction in whole or in part without written permission is strictly
prohibited.

督印人 Publisher	何嘉坤 Tisa Ho
主編 Editor	蘇國雲 So Kwok-wan
執行編輯 Executive Editor	余瑞婷 Susanna Yu
助理編輯 Assistant Editor	王翠屏、李宛虹 Joyce Wong, Lei Yuen-hung
平面設計 排版 Designer	羅美儀 Paula Law
攝影 Photographer	Leo Yu (The Blue Hydrant)
出版 Published by	香港藝術節協會有限公司 Hong Kong Arts Festival Society Limited
印刷 Printer	嘉昱有限公司 Cheer Shine Enterprise Co. Ltd.
版次 Edition	2014 年 2 月初版 1st edition, February 2014
書號 / ISBN	978-988-16056-5-8
定價 / Price	港幣 HK$120
版權垂詢 Copyright Enquiry	香港藝術節協會有限公司 Hong Kong Arts Festival Society Limited

香港灣仔港灣道二號 12 字樓
12/F, 2 Harbour Road, Wan Chai, Hong Kong
電話 Tel　　　: 2824 3555
傳真 Fax　　　: 2824 3798, 2824 3722
網頁 Website : www.hk.artsfestival.org
電郵 Email　 : afgen@hkaf.org

網上追蹤香港藝術節 Follow the HKArtsFestival on www.hk.artsfestival.org
地址 Address : 香港灣仔港灣道 2 號 12 樓 1205 室 Room 1205, 12th Floor, 2 Harbour Road, Wanchai, Hong Kong
電話 Tel : 2824 3555　傳真 Fax : 2824 3798, 2824 3722　電子郵箱 Email : afgen@hkaf.org
節目查詢 (辦公時間內) Programme Enquiries (during office hours) 2824 2430